Greatest Moments in
Football

Greatest Moments in
Football

ROLAND LAZENBY

Page 1: During the Los Angeles-Cleveland NFL Championship
game, the Rams' end Elroy Hirsch blocks a Brown tackler as
'Deacon' Dan Towler goes for a 10-yard gain.
Pages 2-3: In January 1987 Super Bowl XXI pitted the Denver
Broncos against the New York Giants.
This page: The Washington Redskins beat the Chicago Bears,
28-21, in the 1937 Championship game.

CONTENTS

INTRODUCTION

Perhaps more so than anywhere, fame is fleeting in the world of sports. For pro football, today's thrills quickly recede into yesterday and take up residence amidst the yellowed press clippings and faded newsreels. From that pile of yesterday, I've rescued a few of the game's famous moments here, the special plays and magic seasons. I hope you enjoy them. For every occasion listed here, there are probably one hundred others just as deserving of attention. Great tackles and blocks, long forgotten, or if they survive, they live in the memories of old men who played in leather helmets and canvas pants.

The ones here are a smorgasbord of pro football. There are the good old days. Red Grange's grand entry into the game in 1925, the New York Giants' tennis shoe victory of 1934, Sammy Baugh's grand appearance in the league in 1937; the 73-0 whipping George Halas and his Chicago Bears gave the Washington Redskins in 1940. There is the cast of unforgettable characters from the formative years – Steve Van Buren, Paul Brown, Otto Graham, Doak Walker, Bobby Layne, Jim Brown, Bart Starr, Vince Lombardi, Gale Sayers. More recently, there are the superstars of the super age, from Broadway Joe Namath to Roger Staubach to Terry Bradshaw to Joe Montana to Phil Simms. The best and brightest in a game of thuds and thumps, power and finesse, are caught here in all their glory.

Left: In 1984, the Dolphins' Mark Clayton caught a record-breaking 19 touchdown passes.

Below: Green Bay's Jan Stenerud kicks a field goal. In 1983 Stenerud broke George Blanda's career field goal NFL record.

Red Grange and the 1925 Chicago Bears

There are two shapes now moving,
Two ghosts that drift and glide,
And which of them to tackle
Each rival must decide;
They shift with spectral swiftness
Across the swarded range,
And one of them's a shadow,
And one of them is Grange.

Grantland Rice

The legend of Red Grange is fixed in the firmament of sport. Without question, he was the starburst that propelled the dim young galaxy of pro football into a supernova. He was the original bonus baby. The Galloping Ghost. The Wheaton Iceman. But more than anything else, he was The Draw. During the first few weeks of his rookie season in November 1925, Grange's presence generated hundreds of thousands of dollars in gate revenues for the game's uncertain franchises. It is no exaggeration to say Grange lifted pro football from the backlots and fanciful dreams of tinhorn entrepreneurs and part-time players and moved it into the front row of the entertainment business. In a span of 17 days he provided a struggling industry with a glimpse of its brilliant destiny. Seldom has a player accomplished more for a sport in so short a time. Yet for all of Grange's impact on the professional game, he played his best ball in college.

He had gained his strength as a youth toting ice blocks in his hometown of Wheaton, Illinois (thus the name 'The Wheaton Iceman'), but it was Grange's speed, agility and grace that stirred sportswriters and fans. He built his reputation at the University of Illinois with long, elusive runs. Michigan had won 20 straight games until Grange destroyed the Wolverines in the first 12 minutes of their October 1924 match with the Illini. Grange sculpted scoring runs of 95, 56, 67 and 45 yards, moving Grantland Rice to write:

A streak of fire, a breath of flame
Eluding all who reach and clutch;
A gray ghost thrown into the game
That rival hands may rarely touch.

8

Grange scored 31 touchdowns in his 20-game collegiate career and was a three-time Walter Camp All America. In his last college game, played before what was then a record crowd of 85,500, Grange led Illinois to a 14-9 victory over Ohio State.

Two days later he shocked the sports world by signing a contract to begin play immediately for the Chicago Bears. In those days, the pro game had an air of snake oil about it, similar to the image professional wrestling carries today. Not only was it seamy, with athletes playing under aliases, pro football was shaky financially. (That same year Tim Mara had purchased the New York Giants for only $500.)

But the Bears' George Halas figured on Grange's widespread popularity and quickly assembled a barnstorming tour through the East and Midwest. The team played 10 games in 17 days – an incredible pace. Grange finished his college career on Saturday, announced his plans at a Bears' game in Chicago on Sunday, signed a contract on Monday, and played his first pro game the following Thursday, which was Thanksgiving.

The press lamented that America's premier amateur football player had sullied his reputation by turning pro, but the public response was overwhelming. Although most pro games in that era averaged less than 5000 spectators, Halas had the foresight to print 20,000 tickets for the Thanksgiving opener. They were sold in three hours, and Wrigley Field (then known as Cubs Park) was packed with 36,000 fans.

Left: The legendary Red Grange demonstrates his ball-carrying style.
Above right: Grange sits on the bench in his raccoon coat.
Below: Grange signs his contract to play with the Chicago Bears while his agent, C C Pyle (left) and Bears' coach George Halas look on. The Galloping Ghost proved to be a tremendous draw at the gate.

Over the next two and a half weeks, the trains carrying the Bears rolled across the Midwest and East, drawing throngs in each city. The name 'Grange' seemed to mesmerize the public. Despite a downpour, 40,000 fans came out in Philadelphia to see the Galloping Ghost. In New York at the Polo Grounds, 73,000 paid to see the Bears run past the Giants, 19-7. Despite the score, the day was one of New York's winningest, as the $130,000 in gate receipts floated the franchise away from financial disaster.

The breakneck pace made Grange a rich man — his earnings were figured roughly at $300 an hour. But it also left him with a torn muscle and a blood clot in his left arm. He missed a game in Detroit, sending 20,000 fans back to the ticket booth to demand refunds.

After eight days of rest, the team embarked on a second tour, beginning in Miami on Christmas day and winding its way through the South and West. In Los Angeles, 75,000 paid to see the Grange show. After running through 19 games in 17 cities in 66 days, the Bears finished in Seattle 31 January.

Pro football would never be the same after Grange had revealed its grand potential. As for the Ghost, he went on to play for other teams and even started a rival league one year, but a severe knee injury limited his range. He finished his playing days primarily as a defensive player.

For all the hoopla around him, Grange remained genuinely modest. 'Ten years from now,' he said during his playing days, 'no one will know or care what Red Grange did or who he was.'

Nobody said great football players had to be visionaries.

The Bears and Giants: 1933 and 1934 A Comeback Combination

The infant National Football League was up on its feet and toddling in the summer of 1933 when Boston Redskins owner George Preston Marshall got the idea of dividing competition into two divisions.

The result, of course, was the need for a championship game, the league's first. The developments only served to heighten competition and increase the game's popularity. The Chicago Bears and the New York Giants won their divisions over the next two years and served sports fans a hot little rivalry, heavily flavored by fourth-quarter comebacks.

The 1933 game, played at Wrigley Field before 30,000 fans, was a seesaw affair that showcased the battering, running and admirable throwing of Chicago's great 235-pound fullback, Bronko Nagurski. He was aided by the leg of 'Automatic' Jack Manders, who kicked three Bear field goals.

Their performances took the winning edge from the championship effort of New York quarterback Harry Newman, a college All America from Michigan, who completed 12 of 20 passes for 201 yards and two touchdowns.

Late in the fourth quarter, it appeared New York would win, 21-16, until Chicago got the ball back at the Giant 47 after a bad punt. The Bears moved to the 32, then Nagurski threw short to Bill Hewitt. As Hewitt was about to be tackled, he lateralled to end Billy Karr, who streaked 25 yards for the touchdown, the win (23-21) and the trophy.

With the momentum of that first championship game, the Bears rolled through the 1934 season, downing every team in their path, including two victories over New York.

The Giants survived to win their division, but the Bears' dominance seemed complete in the 1934 championship game. More than 35,000 fans at the Polo Grounds watched as Chicago methodically bulled to a 13-3 lead through the third quarter.

The frozen field had left the New York ground game with spinning wheels until the Giants' running backs donned rubber-soled basketball shoes at halftime. Finding their traction as the third period closed, the Giants turned the game into a track meet, scoring 27 points to win 30-13. The stunned Bears seemed helpless spectators.

For all the hype about basketball shoes, much of the credit really belonged to the Giants' inspired offensive line, led by tackle Bill Morgan. First, New York pulled to 13-10 on a 35-yard scoring pass from Ed Danowski to Ike Frankian. Then Ken Strong gave the Giants the lead with a 42-yard scoring run. With Nagurski hampered by injuries, the Bears' response was ineffective. They threw an interception, the Giants scored again and the league had its first 'instant rout'—four touchdowns in less than 15 minutes!

Below: Bear Keith Molesworth runs the ball into Giant territory during the dramatic 9 December 1934 game.
Far right: Redskin quarterback Slingin' Sammy Baugh throws a pass during practice.
Right: Baugh lets go a pass in the 12 December 1937 world title game in which the Redskins downed the Bears, 28-21.

Redskins Triumph
Washington vs. Chicago, 12 December 1937

Just about everything concerning the Washington Redskins was new in 1937. The team had a new name, having moved from Boston to Washington that year. And it had a new passer, 'Slingin' Sam,' Sammy Baugh, fresh out of Texas Christian University and rumored to be the highest paid player in football (with an annual salary somewhere between $7000 and $20,000).

He proved to be worth every nickel of it that year in the NFL Championship game. Like Red Grange before him, Baugh was the type of performer who showed the league its future. He hurled an all-star passing performance into the face of Wrigley Field's withering cold and sent the Bears to defeat, 28-21. Despite the weather, he turned in numbers typical of the pro game of the 1980s – 17 of 34 passes completed for 352 yards and three touchdowns.

Just like Jay Schroeder, Washington's modern quarterback, Baugh had a turn at minor-league baseball before settling into pro football. Baugh had cemented his reputation that summer by leading the College All Stars to a 6-0 victory over the NFL champion Green Bay Packers. Still, Baugh had set his mind on being a major-league shortstop after college. But Skins owner George Preston Marshall sought him out, struggling in the St Louis Cardinals farm system, and talked him into becoming a big-league passer.

The Massacre of 1940
Chicago Bears vs. Washington Redskins

Routs are rarely considered among pro football's great moments. Yet the size and scope of Chicago's 73-0 victory over Washington in the NFL Championship bout on 8 December 1940 make it one of the most astounding pro games ever played. If anything, the outcome emphasized the power of the T-formation offense.

It also said a little something about the importance of coaching and studying game films.

The results were almost unfathomable, considering that Washington, the divisional winner in the East with a 9-2 record, was a 7-5 favorite playing at home. Just three weeks earlier the Redskins had beaten the Bears, 7-3. That earlier victory, in fact, was the rub. With less than a minute to play, the Bears had moved to the Washington one-yard line, only to see time expire without their scoring. They complained bitterly of interference on a final pass play.

Above: The Washington Redskins' end Wayne Millner contributed two touchdowns and three conversions to the Redskins' title victory over the Bears in December of 1937.

GEORGE WILSON

Baugh confirmed Marshall's forecast by turning in one of the great rookie performances of all time. To lift the Skins into the championship match, Baugh had completed 11 of 15 passes a week earlier to defeat New York.

The '37 championship game developed as a classic struggle, with the Bears and Redskins trading touchdowns and the lead through the first half. The decisive offensive moments came in the third quarter, as Baugh shook off a leg injury and guided the Skins to three touchdowns.

The first strike was a 55-yard shot to Wayne Millner. Then a series later, Baugh hit Millner again, this time for 78 yards. That was followed by the decisive toss to Charlie 'Choo-Choo' Justice for 35 yards and the winning margin. For the period, Baugh had completed seven of nine passes for 220 yards.

The Washington defense still needed to deflect three serious Bear drives in the fourth quarter. The battering ram at the heart of the Bears' offense, fullback Bronko Nagurski, was slowed by injuries, and the Redskins held on for the win. That effort and the third quarter scoring outburst earned each of the Redskins their $234.36 championship payoff. It also boosted the legend of Slingin' Sammy.

Left: Chicago Bears end from 1937 to 1946, George Wilson poses for the camera. Wilson's crucial block paved the way for Bill Osmanski's 77-yard scoring run in the beginning of the 1940 championship game.

Top: The Bears' back George McAfee slides off tackle for seven yards in the 1940 NFL Championship game.

Above: Jubilant Bears hold aloft their owner and coach, George Halas, after their 73-0 victory over the Redskins, to win the National Professional Football League title.

When the Washington papers described them as 'crybabies' and Washington owner George Preston Marshall called them a 'first-half ball club,' George Halas and his Bears were bent on vengeance. Upon receiving that opportunity in the championship game, they spent hours preparing.

Halas posted Washington newspaper clippings in the team's locker room and sought the help of Stanford coach Clark Shaughnessy, who had a hand in devising the T-formation. Upon dissecting films of their earlier loss, the Bear coaches realized the Redskins were particularly vulnerable to the counter play. So Chicago packed its offensive game plan with counters.

The Bears received the opening kickoff and on their second offensive play, big Bill 'Bull' Osmanski, their mammoth fullback, took a counter step to his right, then reversed and took the handoff for the left. He found the hole closed inside and slipped outside, heading for the sideline. His size and speed turned the play into a nice gain, but it appeared two Skins safeties would drop him on the Washington 35.

Just then Chicago end George Wilson came from across the field and threw a withering block on both backs, clearing Osmanski's way for a 77-yard scoring run. Speaking with reporters afterward, Halas called it the 'greatest, most vicious block I ever saw.'

Shortly thereafter, the Bears sustained another scoring drive and the rout was on. The first half ended 28-0, and the Bears might have been satisfied to let up the second half, if they hadn't been angered by Marshall's calling them a 'first-half team.' So they added 45 points in the second stanza, piling up the largest total in NFL Championship history.

Crossed up by Crossbars
The Cleveland Rams vs. the Redskins,
17 December 1945

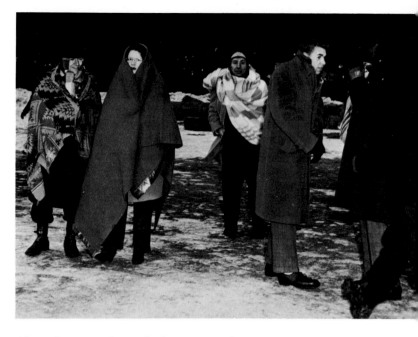

The goalposts played a freakish twelfth man for the Cleveland Rams in the 1945 NFL title game, helping them to edge the Washington Redskins, 15-14. The championship weather was even more dastardly than usual, hovering near zero with gusting winds that sent the chill factor well below that.

The Rams' owner, Dan Reeves, had spent $7500 having 9000 bales of hay spread and tarpaulins over Municipal Stadium field to keep it from freezing. The winter then played its next card, dropping tons of snow the night before the game.

But the weather was just one of the elements holding Washington in a dastardly position. On the opening kickoff, the Redskins' Frank Atkins, the second best ground gainer in the league, broke his nose and was lost for the day. And Washington's great passer, Sammy Baugh, was still hampered by a late-season rib injury.

Early in the first quarter, the Redskins found themselves pinned at their own three-yard line and headed into the gale, as if conditions weren't bad enough. Baugh was working out of a shotgun formation standing in his own end zone.

The goal posts in those days, you may recall, were positioned on the goal line – between Baugh and the playing field. That, however, didn't dent his determination to complete a pass. When end Wayne Millner broke open on a crisscrossing pattern, Baugh was sure he could connect for a touchdown. Instead, the wind lifted the ball into the crossbar and dropped it back, a dead bird, into the end zone. In those days, a pass deflected into the end zone was a safety.

Rather than leading by seven, Washington was down by two. Baugh's rib injury worsened, and he was replaced by Frank Filchock, who directed the Skins to a touchdown and a 7-2 lead. The Rams came right back with a touchdown of their own and again extended their lead by the luck of the goalpost. Bob Waterfield's placement was partially blocked, but the ball struck the crossbar and dropped over. The Rams led, 9-7.

Washington scored again in the third quarter for a brief 14-9 lead. Then the Rams matched that but missed the extra point, leaving them with a slim 15-14 lead. The goalposts that had aided and abetted the opposition became elusive for Washington in the fourth quarter, as the Redskins missed two field goal attempts.

The nasty weather played another role that Sunday, holding down the local crowd and convincing Reeves that he needed to move his team to Los Angeles. Things worked out for the best, as the league expanded west and the upstart Browns were only happy to become Cleveland's team.

Above: Spectators brave the freezing weather to watch the 1945 NFL title game.
Below: Redskins back Dick Todd prepares to knock Rams halfback Fred Gehrke out of bounds as the Rams edge the Redskins, 15-14, to take their first championship.
Below right: Eagles coach Earle 'Greasy' Neale and star player Steve Van Buren discuss strategy.
Below far right: Ram quarterback Van Brocklin is tackled by Eagle Ross Craft during the 1949 National League title game.

Van Buren and Television
The League's First Prime-Time Performance

The 1949 NFL Championship was the precursor of pro football's modern success formula: the league had its first television contract, its leading rusher played the starring role and the game took place in a southern California setting. Yet, as usual, there was an irritating lack of cooperation from the weather.

As things turned out, the 14 December downpour in Los Angeles only served as a framework for showcasing the truly great rushing performance of the Philadelphia Eagles' Steve Van Buren. He had set a league rushing mark of 1146 yards during the 12-game regular season in leading the Eagles to an 11-1 record.

That was enough to make Philadelphia a nine-point favorite to defeat the Los Angeles Rams for the 1949 title. But the Rams' coach, Clark Shaughnessy, had a slick, speedy offense that could break open any game. Still, the unexpected, heavy rains posed questions for everyone, particularly for Commissioner Bert Bell, who had arranged a $30,000 deal with the Dumont Network to televize the game coast-to-coast. That, combined with a radio broadcast arrangement, gave pro football its first multimedia package.

Concerned about ticket sales at the gate, Rams officials phoned Bell in Philadelphia the morning of the game and asked for a one-day delay. The Rams had sold 45,000 advance tickets and hoped to add another 15,000 at the gate. Citing his television deal, Bell refused, and the championship became the slosh-and-slide bowl.

Although he weighed only 208 pounds, Steve Van Buren was the NFL's first great all-purpose back, combining the speed of a tailback with the power of a fullback. He could go inside or outside. 'There was never a player like him,' Philadelphia coach Earle 'Greasy' Neale contended. 'He was better than Red Grange because Grange needed a blocker. Steve didn't. And he could run away from tacklers like Red or over them like Bronko Nagurski.'

For all the talk of a power offense, Neale had to rely on the passing game and his defense to score 14 points in the rain. The Eagles scored in the second quarter on a 31-yard pass from Tommy Thompson to Pete Pihos, then added a security score in the third off a blocked punt.

But it was Van Buren sloshing through the ankle-deep mud behind a powerful offensive line – tackle Al Wistert, center Vic Lindskog and guards Cliff Patton and Bucko Kilroy – that dominated the game. Van Buren carried 31 times for 196 yards, records that would stand for a quarter century.

As Kilroy, the Eagles' guard once said, a great runner comes along once in a decade. Van Buren was the man of the forties.

THE FIFTIES

The Upstart Prevails
The Cleveland Browns vs. the NFL, 1950

The 1950 season brought a classic confrontation of leagues in the merging of the NFL and the four-year-old All-American Football Conference. NFL Commissioner Elmer Layden had been a bit haughty in his comments about the start of a new league. 'Let them get a football,' Layden had remarked in response to overtures that the two leagues merge.

That they did was inevitable. The economics of a young and growing pro football demanded it. The eight-team AAFC had been organized in 1946, with Paul Brown's Cleveland Browns quickly emerging as the dominant team, winning 51 of 58 games and all four league titles. Only three AAFC franchises would survive to join the NFL in 1950. Yet in the incubation of the upstart league, Brown had created a football masterpiece at Cleveland.

The 1950 season would prove that and more as the Browns took the measure of the NFL and captured the championship. The season opener on 16 September was a great one, matching Cleveland against the defending champions, the Eagles.

Brown had selected just the players he wanted to execute his precise passing system. At the heart of the unit was quarterback Otto Graham, whom Brown declared the greatest to ever play the position. Rounding out the machine were Marion Motley at fullback and Mac Speedie and Dante Lavelli in the receiving corps. Needless to say, Brown and his team hadn't been loved by AAFC opponents. Scores ran high as the Browns methodically churned out victories.

The game wasn't a half old before the Eagles got the NFL's first taste of Cleveland's execution. In defense of the Eagles, it should be pointed out that their lineup was decimated. Steve Van Buren, the league's leading rusher, was out with a foot injury, as was halfback Bosh Pritchard. Captain Al Wistert, the heart of the Philly line, was playing hurt.

From start to finish, the game was an Otto Graham air show. He completed 21 of 38 passes for 346 yards and three touchdowns. For measure, Graham also sneaked one over in the fourth quarter, completing a 35-10 route.

Bert Bell, who had replaced Layden as NFL commissioner, conceded the Browns' dominance afterward in the locker room. 'You have as fine a football team as I've ever seen,' he told Paul Brown. The future would bear out that praise, as the Browns played in

seven of the next eight NFL title games.

For 1950, the Browns won the American Conference with a 10-2 record and powered past the New York Giants, 8-3, to face Los Angeles for the league crown on Christmas Eve.

16

Above left: Cleveland Browns' future Hall of Famer coach Paul Brown coached the team from 1946 to 1962.
Left: Browns quarterback Otto Graham receives the Robert J French Memorial Trophy for 'best player in the game' after the 1950 season opener.
Above: Lou Groza kicks the winning field goal for the Browns during the 1950 NFL Championship.

The Rams were not to be taken lightly, having won the National Conference with a 9-3 record and then thumped the Bears 24-14 in the playoffs. Alternating quarterbacks Bob Waterfield and Norm Van Brocklin, they had averaged nearly 40 points a contest in 12 regular season games. Van Brocklin and Waterfield combined for 3709 yards passing, more than 300 per game. They had scored 10 touchdowns against Baltimore and nine against Green Bay. Receiver Tom Fears had caught 84 passes that season.

Although Los Angeles blatantly favored the air game, the team had a stable of excellent running backs – Glenn Davis, Verda Smith, Tom Kalminir, Paul Younger, Dan Towler and Ralph Pasquariello.

While Van Brocklin had injured his ribs in the Chicago game, this Los Angeles offensive machine was geared for a collision with the Browns' defense – the best in the NFL.

Some, including Commissioner Bell, have argued that the 1950 NFL Championship was the greatest ever played. In all, six records would be set and three others tied. On the first offensive play, Davis hesitated as the action went right, then he released from the Ram backfield to the left where he caught a pass and raced 82 yards for the score.

Just 27 seconds had elapsed and the Rams led, 7-0. Graham quickly answered with a 31-yard scoring toss, and the race was on. Los Angeles came right back with a sustained drive for a 14-7 lead. Graham pulled the Browns close again in the second quarter with a 26-yard strike to Lavelli, but the snap on placement was high, and Browns' kicker Lou Groza never got the chance to convert. The Rams led, 14-13, at the half.

Graham opened the third quarter scoring with a 39-yard pass to Lavelli. But then Los Angeles regained the lead, 21-20, with a drive and appeared to ice the game on the next series. Motley fumbled on the Cleveland six, where Larry Brink picked up the ball and ran in for a 28-20 lead.

With five minutes gone in the fourth period, the Browns intercepted a Waterfield pass and began their drive. Converting two fourth-down situations, Graham moved the Browns upfield and connected with Rex Bumgardner for a 19-yard touchdown to bring Cleveland to within one, 28-27.

With two minutes remaining, Waterfield boomed a 51-yard punt into the wind, and Graham started again on his own 32. Mixing running and passing plays and working the sidelines to preserve the clock, Graham pushed the ball to the 10-yard line. There he called time out with 20 seconds left, as Groza calmly walked onto the field with the crowd chanting, and drilled the winning field goal, 30-28.

A last-ditch Ram pass was intercepted, and the Cleveland fans mobbed the field. Aglow in the locker room afterward, Paul Brown told his players, 'This one will be remembered a long time.'

The 1951 NFL Championship

In 1951 Paul Brown's Cleveland machine resumed its domination of the NFL and returned to the championship game by compiling an 11-1 regular season record. Among the Browns' trophies was another set of horns clipped from the Rams, 38-23, during a regular-season rematch of the 1950 title game.

The Rams also returned to the championship, albeit by a more circuitous route, winding their way through the National Conference competition with an 8-4 record. The Los Angeles look for 1951 was new, with a rebuilt offensive line and a shifting in emphasis from the run to the pass. Los Angeles coach Joe Stydahar alternated quarterbacks, veteran Bob Waterfield and youthful Norm 'Dutch' Van Brocklin.

A year would make a big difference, particularly for Van Brocklin, who had played little in the 1950 championship because of a rib injury. Van Brocklin's favorite weapon was the long pass, with the emphasis on long. It would be his and the Rams' saving grace in December 1951. They also had a new force on the defensive line – end Andy Robustelli – who would team with Larry Brink to outduel Cleveland's veteran offensive front and handcuff Otto Graham's passing game.

As it was, the teams were matched evenly. After a scoreless first quarter, LA tallied first on a one-yard run by Dick Hoerner. Cleveland answered with a 52-yard field goal from Lou Groza and a 17-yard touchdown pass from Graham to take a 10-7 halftime lead. In the third quarter the tide shifted as Waterfield directed the Rams to a touchdown and a 14-10 Los Angeles lead. Late in the third quarter, Graham threw a touchdown pass, but the play was called back on a holding penalty against Groza. When the Browns were forced to punt to start the fourth period, Van Brocklin was sent into the game for the first time.

On successive series, the young quarterback moved his team to the Browns' one-yard line, and each time Cleveland snuffed the threat with inspired goal-line defense. On the second drive, Waterfield kicked a 17-yard field goal, extending the Rams' lead, 17-10. That seemed to awaken Graham and the Browns, who drove 70 yards to tie the score after the ensuing kickoff – all the while Van Brocklin was fuming and stomping along the sidelines.

The Rams' go-ahead effort seemed stalled when their first two plays gained only three yards. But Van Brocklin, an intuitive reader of defenses, had noticed the Browns' defensive backs were vulnerable in the middle. So he had receiver Tom Fears cut there from a sideline pattern. The pass nestled into Fears' outstretched hands as he split two defenders for a 73-yard touchdown, a play perfect for history. Leading 24-17, the Rams turned to their defense, which flexed, stifled Cleveland's last drive and wrapped up Los Angeles' championship. What you might call a 'Dutch' treat.

Above left: Rams quarterback Bob Waterfield gets flipped skyward by Browns Darrell Palmer during their 1951 NFL Championship game, which the Rams won, 27-14.
Below left: Rams end Elroy 'Crazy Legs' Hirsch reaches to snare a pass on the Browns' 37-yard line during the 1951 NFL Championship game.
Above: Cleveland coach Paul Brown crouches on the sidelines with two of his players.
Below: Jubilant Rams celebrate their 24-17 victory over the Browns, which gave them the 1951 NFL crown.
Right: The Lions' halfback Doak Walker contributed a touchdown, two conversions and a field goal to his team's 1953 championship victory over the Browns.

The Motor City Takes to The Passing Layne
Detroit Downs The Browns, 27 December 1953

The early 1950s would have belonged to the Cleveland Browns if it hadn't been for this other little team across Lake Erie, the Detroit Lions. In their short tenure in the NFL, the Browns had ruled the league, except for the Lions, who had not lost to Cleveland since the 1950 exhibition season.

The power of the Lions rested with the competitiveness of quarterback Bobby Layne and the running and kicking of halfback Doak Walker, both of them Texas boys who had played on the same high school team. They had gone to separate colleges, Walker to SMU, Layne to the University of Texas. But they had reunited in the pros to lead Detroit to a 17-7 victory over the Browns in the 1952 championship game. Then, despite a few miscues along the way, they repeated the act and guided the Lions back for a rematch in 1953.

From the outset of the season, the Browns, fired by Paul Brown's desire, seemed primed to smash their way right to the championship. They won their first 11 games, including a 62-14 humiliation of the

rival New York Giants, and claimed the divisional title handily. Cleveland seemed invincible in taking a 21-0 lead over Philadelphia in the last regular-season game. Suddenly the Eagles came alive and buried the Browns, 42-27, in one of the most startling comebacks in NFL history.

The game, however, is merely a footnote, for the Browns had already claimed the division and were headed for the title game with Detroit. The real impact of the loss to the Eagles was that it left a cloud of doubt in Cleveland's confidence.

For their part, the Lions had dallied a bit before winning their division with a 10-2 record. But they had finished strong and carried their momentum into the championship on their home field, Detroit's Briggs Stadium.

All in all, the 1953 game was marked by tremendous defense. But as always seems the case, the golden moments fell to the quarterbacks and receivers, and like any great NFL quarterback, Layne was eager for the gold.

On the down side, either quarterback – Layne or Cleveland's Otto Graham – could have worn the goat's horns that day. Both contributed their share of turnovers leading to opponent's scores. The game opened with Lions rookie linebacker Joe Schmidt nailing Graham and forcing a fumble inside the Browns' 20. The Lions battered the ball in after several plays, with Walker scoring on a one-yard dive, then kicking the conversion.

The Browns got a similar opportunity in the second quarter when they recovered a fumble at the Detroit six. But the defense held, and Cleveland was resigned to a Lou Groza field goal.

It was a miserable day for Graham, the league's leading passer who had completed better than 62 percent of his passes during the regular season. His performance changed completely in the championship. The Lions sacked and befuddled the normally unshakeable Graham into connecting on only 2 of 15 attempts for 31 yards. While he struggled, Detroit forged ahead, as Walker added a field goal, giving Detroit a 10-3 halftime lead.

The Cleveland players were steamed in a scathing talk from Brown at intermission, which was enough to reverse the tide in the third quarter. Layne contributed two turnovers to the Browns' effort. First, he threw an interception, which led to Cleveland's drive to tie the score. Then at the end of the quarter, Layne fumbled, the Browns recovered and Groza kicked a field goal for a 13-10 lead.

With 4:10 to play, Groza added another field goal for a 16-10 lead that seemed solid on a day dominated by defenses. It was the type of challenge Layne thrived on.

Detroit's hopes for an offensive resurgence were dimmed by the loss of all-star end Leon Hart in the first half. His substitute was Jim Doran, a converted defensive back who had been the team's MVP the year before but had played little during the last half of the

Above: Officials debate the legality of a Lions touchdown during the 1953 championship game. The touchdown was not good because of an illegal forward pass.
Right: Lion end Jim Doran catches a Layne pass for a 20-yard gain in the 1953 NFL Championship game. This gain set up the Lions' winning touchdown.

'53 season. Doran and Browns defensive back Warren Lahr had tussled through the second half, a confrontation that would become the focus of Detroit's last-ditch drive.

Starting at his own 20, Layne drove the Lions with a series of passes to Doran. Quickly, the Lions found themselves at the Cleveland 33 with a first down, a perfect setting for surprise. Lions coach Buddy Parker wanted a screen pass, but Doran came to the huddle pleading for a chance to beat Lahr long. Layne listened.

On the snap, Doran headed at Lahr as if to block him, then bolted long with a yard lead on the Browns defender. The pass was there for a 33-yard touchdown, just one of the many completions that nailed down Layne's reputation as the original comeback quarterback. It also helped reserve him a place in the Hall of Fame. The home crowd roared that day as Walker came on the field to kick the extra point, for a 17-16 Detroit lead.

The Lions' work wasn't finished, however, until Carl Karilivacz intercepted Graham's last pass and killed Cleveland's drive. The Browns, as the saying goes, would have to wait until next year, which they did, resoundingly thumping the Lions, 56-10, for the '54 championship.

But the moment, the '53 comeback, the championship, belonged to the Lions and two high school boys from Texas.

Bombs Away
Detroit Surprises the 49ers,
22 December 1957

Things seemed impossible for the Detroit Lions before the 1957 season. Or at least coach Buddy Parker thought so. 'I can't handle a losing season,' he told reporters. 'This team of ours is the worst I've ever seen in training. I'm leaving Detroit . . . tonight.'

Assistant coach George Wilson took over, and somehow Detroit moved along, staying in contention for the title. Then, with two games remaining, the Lions faced another setback – the loss of quarterback Bobby Layne to a leg injury.

With substitute Tobin Rote at quarterback, Detroit tied San Francisco for the Western Conference regular season title (both teams had 8-4 records). But San Francisco – with YA Tittle at quarterback, Hugh McElhenny in the backfield and RC Owens at receiver – was the favorite for the playoffs. The 49ers were playing at home, in Kezar Stadium, before a crowd of nearly 60,000. Without Layne, Detroit's main offensive weapon was running back Tom 'the Bomb' Tracy. But the public sentiment was that Detroit would get bombed, rather than turn any loose.

Instead of rising to the occasion, the Lions played to Parker's prediction in the first half. Using the 'Alley-Oop' pass the 49ers made famous, Tittle connected with Owens for a 34-yard touchdown and a quick, 7-0 San Francisco lead. Minutes later, Tittle hit McElhenny releasing from the backfield, and the great back cut and shifted his way to a 47-yard score.

Down 14-0, the Lions momentarily found their offensive stride. Rote threw Steve Junker a three-yard touchdown pass to pull Detroit to 14-7. The 49ers answered with Tittle's third touchdown pass for a 21-7 lead. After Gordy Soltau added a field goal right before the half, San Francisco team officials seemed comfortable enough with a 24-7 lead to announce the sale of championship game tickets over the stadium public address system. Smarting, the Lions sat in their locker room where through the walls they could hear the 49ers beginning their celebration early.

The insult immediately deepened as McElhenny took the second half kickoff and spun his way to the Lions' nine-yard line before being tackled by Detroit's great defensive halfback, Yale Lary. In that dark moment, backed up against their goal line, facing a rout, the Lions turned tough, and allowed the 49ers only a field goal for a 27-7 lead.

From that point on, the San Francisco offense resembled a train stalled on a hill. On the next series, Tittle fumbled on his own 28. The Lions recovered, and nine plays later, Tracy rammed in for a score, bringing the tally to 27-14. The Lions' defense held, but when the offense got the ball back, it went nowhere. Then came the call of the decade. Facing fourth down on his own 20, George Wilson told Rote

Above: Four sequence shots depict the action during the 1957 NFL Western Division title playoff game. San Francisco 49er R C Owens catches a Tittle pass, then breaks out of James David's hold and scores the 49ers' first touchdown.
Left: Lion substitute fullback Tom Tracy breaks clear for a third-quarter 58-yard touchdown run during the 22 December 1957 playoff game. The Lions overcame a 20-point deficit to win the division title by a 31-27 margin.
Next page: Lion guard James Martin kicks the winning field goal in the 1957 Lions-49ers division title playoff game.

to pass instead of punt.

The gamble worked, with Rote throwing to Howard 'Hopalong' Cassidy for 14 yards and a first down. Moments later, Tracy exploded on a weaving, exhilarating 58-yard touchdown run. The score was 27-21, with almost three minutes left in the third quarter.

The 49ers, it seemed, had fixed their minds on the clock, as they relinquished the ball again after three downs. The quarter ended with Detroit driving for the go-ahead touchdown. That came with not quite a minute gone in the fourth period, on a two-yard run by Gene Gedman. The Lions led, 28-27, and the 49ers came apart, first with a fumble, then an interception.

Tracy also fizzled a Detroit drive with a fumble at San Francisco's three-yard line. But the Lions got yet another interception, and after the 49ers' defense

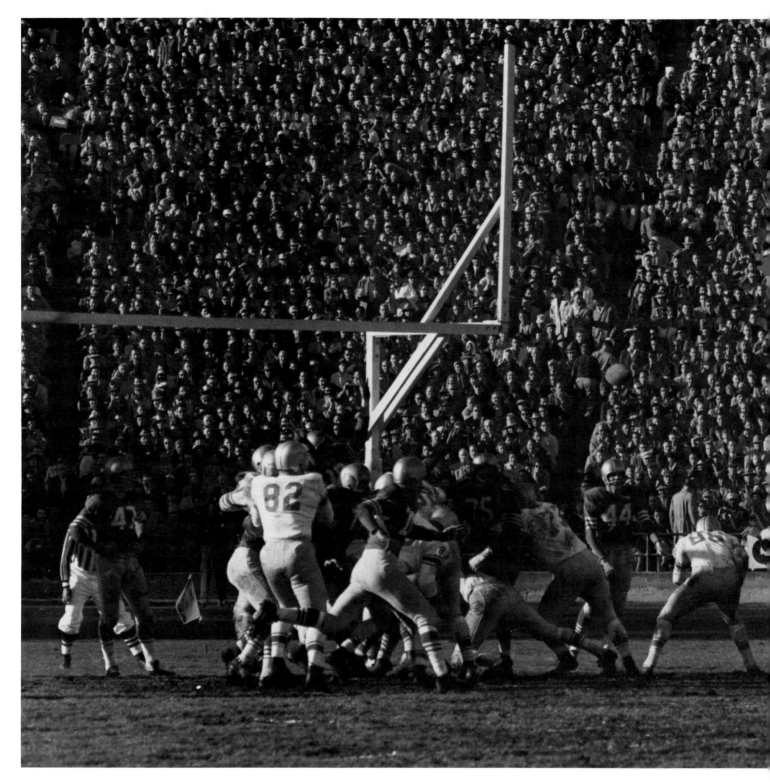

held, Jim Martin kicked a field goal for a 31-27 lead.

His comfortable lead having vanished in the December air, Tittle found himself running a hurry-up offense with two minutes left and no timeouts remaining. Showing the savvy that would make him a Hall of Famer, the 49er quarterback moved his team to the Lions' 49 with a minute left. But then the Lions' defensive end Darris McCord sacked Tittle, which in turn was followed by another tackle for a loss, and the San Francisco threat was ended.

After that, Detroit had a little date with destiny and the Cleveland Browns, whose offense featured a brilliant rookie running back, Jim Brown. With Brown leading the league in rushing yards (942), the rebuilt Browns had finished the regular season 9-2-1. Brown had set the single-game rushing record against the Rams that year (237 yards in 31 attempts).

The offensive spotlight, however, belonged to Rote that day. The Detroit sub threw four touchdown passes and ran for another as the Lions obliterated

The Greatest Game?
Colts vs. The Giants,
28 December 1958

NFL Commissioner Bert Bell was so pleased with the 1958 championship that he called it the greatest football game ever played. It wasn't long before nearly everybody was saying that. History and 1000 subsequent NFL games may have tempered that appraisal a bit, but it was one fine athletic event. Perhaps you could call it the 'greatest' game in the same way you might call Red Grange football's 'greatest' player. He was outstanding and his contribution to the spectacle of the sport remains unsurpassed by any single player.

Likewise, the 1958 championship contributed far more than any other game to the spectacle of the sport. After all, it was the league's very first sudden-death overtime championship, broadcast to nail-biting football fans around the world. It revealed a new, exciting edge to this old game of thuds and thumps.

The cast involved many of the truly great ones. Tom Landry and Vince Lombardi were assistants to Giant coach Jim Lee Howell. Alex Webster and Frank Gifford were residents of the New York backfield, along with grizzled Charlie Conerly at quarterback. Pat Summerall was the place kicker. But that was merely the offensive unit. The rocks in New York's ribs were defenders: Sam Huff and Cliff Levingston at linebacker; Dick Modzelewski and Rosey Grier at tackle; Andy Robustelli at end; Jimmy Patton and Emlen Tunnell in the secondary. Landry was the mind behind the monster, aligning this talent in a 4-3 that flexed and crushed opponents, creating a resurgence in New York football that filled the throngs in Yankee Stadium with raving, noisy madness each home game. 'Defense!' the Giant crowd repeatedly roared.

Defense Landry gave them. The Giants had given up a league-low 183 points and outlasted Cleveland three times to win the Eastern Conference title.

The Colts? They were led by a nearly anonymous supernova, John Unitas, a ninth-round draft pick out of basketball country, the University of Louisville, who had been cut by the Pittsburgh Steelers and wound up playing semipro ball for the Bloomfield Rams (in Pittsburgh) for $6 a week. Somehow the Colts dug him up when their regular, George Shaw, was injured, and watched Johnny U become the league MVP for 1957. He was still a reasonably well kept secret by the '58 title game. Until then, no one realized he could work absolute magic.

Nevertheless, Baltimore was anything but a one-man show. Rangy and precise, Raymond Berry was the wide receiver and Unitas' main target. LG Dupre and Alan 'The Horse' Ameche were the power in the backfield. Lenny Moore was the philly, the flanker/halfback, the gamebreaker.

The Colts played a little defense, too, with Gino

Cleveland, 59-14, for the NFL championship. Each player on the championship team earned $4,295.41; the losers each received $2,750.31.

It was quite an accomplishment for a group of players who had been dismissed by their coach as losers. As for Parker, he accepted the head coaching job at Pittsburgh and finished the year with a 6-6 record.

The Lions, it seems, had rephrased an adage: He who celebrates last, celebrates best.

Marchetti at end, Gene 'Big Daddy' Lipscomb at tackle, Don Shinnick and Bill Pellington backing the line – and nasty, naughty Johnny Sample in the secondary. Combined, they were team enough for a 9-3 record and the Western championship over Chicago.

Still, New York had won the regular-season contest between the two teams, and Baltimore hadn't beaten the Giants since 1954.

Furthermore, the setting for their epic collision was Yankee Stadium, filled with 64,175 truly lucky fans lusting for the thud of the Giants' defense. A few million more tuned in on television.

The first quarter brought them the slightest taste of offense, as neither team could gain a first down in the opening 10 minutes. Finally, New York sustained a drive, only to see it gasp and die on the Colts' 36, from where Summerall kicked a field goal.

The Colts cracked their scoreboard goose egg in the second quarter, after Big Daddy Lipscomb recovered a Gifford fumble (he was to lose the ball three times in the quarter) inside the New York 20-yard line. Baltimore hammered into the end zone on a series of dives, with Ameche going the final two yards for a 7-3 lead.

Toward the close of the half, the Giants again threatened, but Gifford lost a second fumble, this time inside the Baltimore 15-yard line. The Colts recovered and began another grinding march. Using mostly running plays, Unitas directed the Colts to the New York 15. There he zipped a pass to Berry in the end zone. With a 14-3 halftime advantage, the Colts were able to take some of the zeal out of the home crowd.

Above left: Quarterback Charles Conerly played for the Giants from 1948 to 1961.
Above: Colt quarterback Johnny Unitas threw 26 completions for 349 yards to propel his team to victory in the 1958 NFL Championship.
Right: Charley Conerly throws as the Colts' Gino Marchetti tries to block the pass during the 1958 Giants-Colts NFL Championship.

The numbness deepened in the third quarter as Baltimore drove to the Giants' three-yard line, where Landry's unit dug in. For three downs, the defense held. On fourth down, Colts coach Weeb Ewbank disdained a field goal and went for six points. The Giants repelled Ameche and started their comeback.

'We talked about it [a field goal],' Ewbank told reporters afterward, 'but I wanted to bury them right there with a touchdown.'

Indeed, the Giants clawed their way out of the grave. Two running plays moved the ball to the 13, where Conerly threw deep to veteran receiver Kyle Rote. Caught from behind at the Colt 25, Rote fumbled. Alex Webster, who was trailing the play, scooped up the ball and advanced it to the Baltimore one. On the next play, Mel Triplett punched in for the score. After Summerall's conversion, the Giants trailed 14-10, and the crowd had regained its lustiness.

Landry's defense did its job throughout the remainder of the period, and the fourth quarter opened with the Giants driving for the go-ahead score. With less than a minute gone in the period, Gifford caught a 15-yard touchdown pass, and New York regained the lead, 17-14. The darkness that descended on the late afternoon couldn't have been more figurative for the Colts. The stadium lights were turned on as they set up to receive the kickoff.

Again Landry's unit prevailed, dousing two Baltimore drives and giving the offense the opportunity to control the ball and the game with a late drive to beat the clock. Facing a third and four at the New York 40, Conerly called for Gifford to power off tackle.

Gifford, better known today as an ABC-TV broadcaster, still swears that he made it. Gino Marchetti and Lipscomb were the stoppers for Baltimore. Gifford seemed to nudge past the first-down marker, but veteran head linesman Charley Berry and referee Ron Gibbs assessed the forward progress and moved the ball back to where they saw Gifford downed. When the pile was untangled, Marchetti was carried from the field with a fractured leg, and New York was inches short of the first down. The crowd, of course, howled otherwise.

Howell had little choice but to punt, the Giant kicker Don Chandler responded with a beauty, pinning the Colts at their 14 with 1:56 left. 'I was sure then it was all over,' Lombardi said afterward.

But Unitas found a spark and turned it into a flame. On third and 10, he passed to Lenny Moore for a first down at the 25. Then came three brilliant completions to Berry, first a slant up the middle for 25 yards, followed by a diving reception at the 35 and finished by a quick hook at the 13.

With 0:07 left, kicker Steve Myhra calmly entered the game and tied the score at 17. The numbness again descended on the New York crowd. This sudden-death overtime stuff was new territory, even in the Big Apple.

'We were so damn disgusted with ourselves that when we got the ball for that last series, we struck back at the Giants in a sort of blind fury,' Unitas said afterward of the drive to tie the game.

His magic, however, drooped briefly as he made a bad call on the coin toss for overtime. New York won and elected to receive. After three plays, the Giants still needed a yard for a first down, so Chandler again punted beautifully. The Colts took over on their 20, and Unitas started them down the field into history.

To minimize the chances of a turnover, he kept the ball on the ground. Dupre ran for 11 yards, then after two failed dives, Unitas gambled and shot a flare pass to Ameche in the flats, and The Horse bulled to another first down. The progress was halted momentarily when Modzelewski lanced through the heart of the pocket and sacked Unitas for an eight-yard loss. Looking at third and long, Unitas executed what the analysts came to savor as the game's most crucial play. First, he dropped to pass, hesitated, then broke to the left seemingly headed for the end, then stopped, faked a pass, then faded farther out. Berry, shaking and darting, broke open when Giant halfback Carl

Karilivacz stumbled. Still, Unitas hesitated, motioning for Berry to go farther. Finally satisfied, he zipped the ball 21 yards to Berry's wide target, number 82, for another first down at the New York 42. The unsung heroes of that great moment were the Colts' offensive linemen – George Preas, Buzz Nutter and company – who kept Unitas free for a leisurely scramble.

With the Giants plump for the fall, Unitas called the draw to Ameche. It went for 22 yards and another first down just inside the Giants' 20. The New York defense tightened and stopped a run for a yard gain. But Unitas threw to Berry at the eight.

On the verge of football's great moment with nearly everyone in Yankee Stadium sensing an imminent field goal, a fan broke loose from the crowd and headed onto the field. Play was stopped for a full minute until police could entice him back into the stands. Unitas watched calmly, then crossed up the defense again when play resumed, throwing a sideline pass to tight end Jim Mutscheller, who went out of bounds at the one-yard line.

The next call was a dive to Ameche. The hole was wide, to say the least, and instead of defenders, The Horse was greeted by joyous Baltimore fans who rushed the end zone to greet him.

'When I slapped the ball into Ameche's belly and saw him take off,' Unitas told reporters, 'I knew nobody was gonna stop him.'

28

The fans wrested away the game ball, and several Colts chased them down to retrieve it. Lost momentarily in the stupendous celebration were the statistics. Unitas had completed 26 of 40 passes for 349 yards. Berry had caught 12 for 178 yards. The Giants, alas, had set a record with six fumbles. Soon after the roar grew to a din, the Colts retired to the locker room to savor their winners' checks – $4718.77 apiece.

The game, this 'greatest of all,' propelled the league toward a financial future that it, too, could savor. As for the Colts, they had earned a championship, not just one for 1958. This one was for the ages.

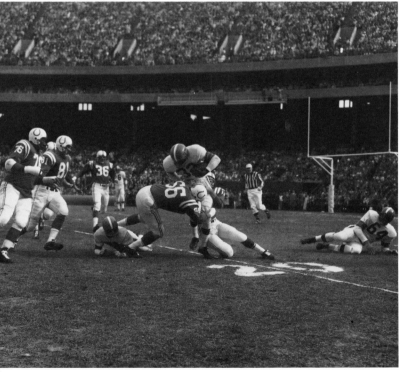

Offensive Cameo
Cleveland Browns vs. Baltimore Colts, 1 November 1959

It was a November game in a season that would go nowhere special for the Cleveland Browns. Their opponents, the Baltimore Colts, would go on to crush the New York Giants that December of 1959 for their second straight NFL championship.

This game, played 1 November in Baltimore, was little more than a cameo, a gem of an exhibition by two of the era's most storied offensive performers: Cleveland's Jim Brown and the Colts' Johnny Unitas.

Leading into the game, the press had made much of a third factor, Baltimore's 6'6", 300-pound defensive tackle, Gene 'Big Daddy' Lipscomb, who had told reporters before the game that he'd been 'waiting a long time to get my hands on that Cleveland cat.'

Far more than a cat, Brown was a lion, an immortal mix of speed and power, grace and guile. Arguably, he was the greatest running back ever. In 1959 he was in the middle of a streak of leading the NFL in rushing for five straight years. After a year's interlude in 1962 when Green Bay's Jim Taylor would lead the league, Brown would resume his dominance, running farther than any other back for another three years.

Unitas, of course, was basking in public adulation, having led the Colts to the championship the year before and on his way to taking them there again in 1959.

So the game became a contest, the Big Gun versus the Big Run.

Brown took the Lipscomb factor as an extra challenge. Through the first half, the Cleveland fullback ran repeatedly at the Colts' tackle, so much so that as the teams broke for the half Lipscomb accused Brown of trying to make fun of him. 'I'm gonna get you in the second half,' Big Daddy warned.

The confrontation, however, never developed, as Brown continued his onslaught, piling up 176 yards and five touchdowns, 'one of the greatest performances ever,' according to Cleveland coach Paul Brown.

For his part, Unitas did nothing to hurt his own legend, passing for 397 yards and four touchdowns. It just wasn't enough to offset Brown, as Cleveland won, 38-31.

As time wound down, the fans in Baltimore gave Brown a standing ovation. And afterward, in the Colts' locker room, Lipscomb added his own acknowledgement.

'I'm still waiting,' Big Daddy told reporters, 'to get my hands on that cat.'

Above, far left: Alan Ameche scores the winning touchdown during overtime to give his Colts the 1958 NFL Championship.
Top left: Pittsburgh Steeler Gene 'Big Daddy' Lipscomb.
Left: Cleveland fullback Jim Brown is brought down during the 1 November 1959 game.

The American Dream: A New League, 1960

As most rival leagues had before it, the American Football League initiated play in 1960 with a mix of castoffs, tired talents and second chancers. Here and there, amid the crowd, a nugget of legitimate big-league ability would glisten.

Yet whatever the individual assessments, the young teams made a beginning that year, and from it would grow a unit of style and savvy that would eventually meld with the NFL, bringing the old league a new look, a new color, a new energy. The results would be Super.

But that's getting ahead of the story. In actuality, the AFL was started because two Texas boys – Lamar Hunt in Dallas and Kenneth S 'Bud' Adams in Houston – couldn't persuade the NFL owners to grant them franchises.

It was a rush to get teams organized and games scheduled. For the snobs, the AFL was definitely a backlot league in 1960. Real football connoisseurs, however, knew a thrill when they felt it. If nothing else, these awkward young teams were entertaining. On occasion, they were even sophisticated.

Of course, ABC helped things tremendously by offering a five-year television contract worth nearly $9 million; it was the first trickle in a soon-to-be tide of media money aimed at promoting and developing professional football. So the bills, for the most part, were paid. And the teams, despite speculation to the contrary, survived.

As was expected, a bidding skirmish broke out immediately, the first one coming over LSU's Heisman winner, Billy Cannon, who signed contracts with both Los Angeles of the NFL and Houston of the AFL. Pete Rozelle challenged Cannon's plans to go with Houston, but the courts decided in Houston's favor.

In retrospect, NFL partisans might concede that the new league made great gains for pro football by opening markets in new places such as Denver, Oakland, Buffalo and Houston (the infatuation would later spread to Miami, Kansas City and San Diego), or reestablishing them in Dallas and Boston, or blatantly challenging the NFL in Los Angeles and New York.

It helped that the first game, played 9 September, was an upset. But that's about all you could honestly say for it. Speed, power, precise blocking and crisp tackling – all were absent. Underdog Denver came back to defeat Boston, 13-10, with no-names such as Carmichael, Tripucka, Mingo and Colclough doing the scoring.

Later, the first championship game, between Houston and Los Angeles, would feature old NFL hand George Blanda flinging bombs. Billy Cannon would haul in a Blanda aerial for an 88-yard score to ice Houston's 24-16 victory.

A new brand of football was on its way.

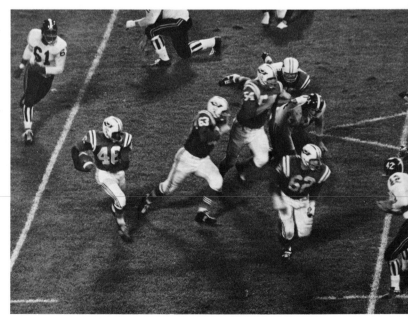

Bednarik and the Benchmark Championship
Philadelphia Eagles vs. Green Bay Packers, 26 December 1960

Adying era collided with the future of football in the 1960 NFL Championship, and for a special moment, the elder prevailed, making one last statement about its manhood and toughness, before closing its chapter forever, taking with it a final trophy.

The unexpected ushers at this changing of the gridiron guard were the Philadelphia Eagles, who had wallowed in mediocrity since their championship appearances in 1948 and 1949. After winning the 1960 title, they would again disappear into the NFL pack for two more decades.

The old era of pro football was epitomized by the Eagles' Chuck Bednarik, the last of the two-way players, a 35-year-old center-linebacker of immense toughness. He played the full 60 minutes of the title game, and the outcome would prove that he was needed to the very last second.

The NFL's new tomorrow was the Green Bay Packers of coach Vince Lombardi, making the first of their six championship appearances. They were future Hall of Famers, on the verge of their greatness: Bart Starr, Jim Taylor, Paul Hornung, Max McGee, Ray Nitschke, Forrest Gregg, Willie Davis and company.

Coming as an assistant from New York in 1959, Lombardi had taken over a 1-10-1 team. 'Gentlemen,' he told his players, 'I have never been associated with a losing team, and I do not intend to start now.' They finished 7-5 that year, and by the next season, they had played their way to the championship.

The Eagles, on the other hand, were a loose collection of veterans and rookies, who to the surprise of

Far left: Former Notre Dame coach Frank Leahy (left) chats with AFL Commissioner Joe Foss (center) and AFL founder and Dallas Texans President Lamar Hunt (right) during the 1960 Patriots-Texans exhibition game.
Left: The Boston Patriots' halfback Larry Garran drives for a gain during the 1960 season opener in which the underdog Broncos downed the Pats.
Above: Eagles Norm Van Brocklin unleashes a pass against Green Bay during the 1960 NFL Championship.
Right: Green Bay's Ray Nitschke bears down on Eagles end Bob Walston during the 1960 NFL Championship game.

the rest of the league, jelled as a team and played beyond their potential. They were led by Norm Van Brocklin at quarterback and receiver Tommy McDonald and sparked by rookie running back Ted Dean.

The two teams met in the 1960 NFL championship game on 26 December. Despite their youth, the Packers gained most of the yardage and reaped a bushel of Philly turnovers. Only in points, only where it really mattered, did they fall short. About nine yards short, to be exact.

Green Bay quickly seized the momentum by intercepting a lateral at the Eagles' 14 on Philadelphia's first offensive series. The Packers rammed the ball down to the 6, where Bednarik and the Eagle defense held, setting the tone for the rest of the afternoon.

Philadelphia began a drive from its own five, but Dean fumbled three plays later. The Packers took over on the 22. Alternating Hornung and Taylor, Green Bay battered to the 13, where two passes failed, and Lombardi reluctantly signaled for the field goal. Hornung was true, and the Packers led, 3-0.

The second quarter produced two more deep penetrations by Green Bay, but the Eagle defense allowed only another field goal. 'We lost the game right there,' Lombardi told reporters afterward. 'Instead of leading 14-0, it was only 6-0.'

The tide then shifted before the half, as Van Brocklin found McDonald for a 35-yard scoring pass. A series later, Philadelphia sustained another drive to the Green Bay 15, where a Bobby Walston field goal made it 10-6. With time running out in the half, Starr drove the Packers from their 20 to the Eagles' 14, where Hornung attempted a field goal from a difficult angle. He missed.

The third quarter was a classic defensive stand-off, marked by Bednarik's crunching tackle that removed Hornung from action with a pinched nerve. The Packers opened the fourth quarter with a scoring drive, made complete by a seven-yard scoring toss from Starr to McGee with 13:07 left. Green Bay's 13-10 lead was immediately threatened as Dean returned the kickoff to the Packers' 39. The Eagles then drove to the five, where Dean completed the job he started on the kickoff by scoring on the next play, giving Philadelphia a 17-13 lead.

The Packers then suffered three false starts getting out of the blocks. Bednarik snuffed one drive with a fumble recovery. Two other Green Bay possessions died on downs. Finally, Starr was given one last opportunity, getting the ball back on his own 35 with 1:30 left. It was a masterful drive that came to its climax on the Eagles' 22 with just 17 seconds and no Green Bay timeouts left.

There, the old and new collided, the old being Bednarik, playing the last few seconds of his 60 minutes; the new being Jim Taylor, the Packers' bullish young fullback, who had just pulled in an outlet pass at the line of scrimmage after Starr had been unable to find an open receiver in the end zone.

Taylor broke through several defenders and found only Bednarik at the nine-yard line between him and the championship. The game clock favored the old, but time favored the new. Bednarik executed a masterful tackle and then lay on top of Taylor, who was fussing and twisting to get up, until the last seconds ran off the clock and Philadelphia had won.

It was a golden way to close a career, an era.

Bednarik was 'one of the real pros,' Green Bay end Gary Knafelc said afterward. 'He's one of the toughest men I've ever met.'

Only in Texas
The AFL Championship,
Dallas vs. Houston, 23 December 1962

The AFL got a much needed transfusion of thrill with its 1962 championship game between the Dallas Texans and Houston Oilers. As with the pivotal 1958 NFL championship, this one was also played before a nationwide television audience. And just like the 1958 game, this one went to sudden-death overtime. Make that double sudden-death overtime.

Pro football's second championship tie breaker lasted most of six periods, until Dallas rookie placekicker Tommy Brooker nailed a 25-yarder with 2:54 left in the second overtime to give the Texans the title with a 20-17 win. The 37,981 fans in Houston's Jeppesen Stadium were held captive by the outcome and dampened by a drizzle throughout the long afternoon. As much as anything, the game was a battle against the elements, as both teams were slowed by loose, muddy turf and befuddled by gusting winds.

Comic relief was provided by Dallas' running back Abner Haynes, who miscalled the overtime coin toss, giving the Oilers the ball and the advantage of the wind to start the sudden death.

Regulation play was as perfectly symmetrical as any football game can be. The Dallas offense, guided by quarterback Len Dawson, racked up 17 points in the first half. Then in the second half George Blanda pushed the Oilers through their paces to match that, leaving the game hinging on his 42-yard field goal attempt as time expired. Dallas linebacker Sherrill Headrick blocked it, and the damp fans settled down for the extra period.

With a weak kicking game, Texas coach Hank Stram had wanted to open the overtime on defense to prevent his offense from getting pinned deep in its own territory facing the wind. He told Haynes that if Houston won the toss, Dallas would kick to the clock and defend with the wind.

Haynes became confused when Dallas won the toss and told the referee, 'We'll kick to the clock,' which gave Houston the wind and the ball. The Oilers hooted at the mistake, but wasted their opportunity with two interceptions and failed to score in the first overtime.

The Texans opened the second overtime with the ball and the wind and used that advantage to sail downfield to the 25, where finally Brooker complied with his championship kick.

He was a happy young rookie – but not nearly as happy as Abner Haynes.

Far left: The Eagles' Tommy McDonald after scoring a touchdown in the NFL Championship game.
Middle left: Dallas Texans quarterback Len Dawson was the AFL's passing leader in 1960.
Left: George Blanda, the Houston Oilers' veteran quarterback from 1960 to 1966.

No Title for Tittle
Chicago vs. N Y Giants,
29 December 1963

In 1961, after playing 13 seasons with Baltimore and San Francisco, YA Tittle was traded to the hastily rebuilt New York Giants, where his career gained a new momentum. For three seasons, he laced Eastern Conference opponents with touchdown passes. In 1962 he threw 33 scoring strikes to lead the league, and the next year he retained the crown by throwing a league-record 36.

Three times he led the Giants to the NFL Championship game, and three times Tittle was denied. It seemed that when he needed touchdown passes the most, he couldn't find the range. His last trip to the title game, in 1963 when he was known as the 37-year-old 'Bald Eagle,' was perhaps his most frustrating, because victory was closest to his grasp.

With the championship dancing just out of his reach, he fought off injury and interceptions with a memorable effort. While he didn't win in the bitter cold of Chicago's Wrigley Field on 29 December 1963, Tittle offered the sports world ample evidence of his great undefeated spirit.

In the 1961 championship game, the Green Bay Packers had hammered New York, 37-0. Then the next year they salted the Giants' wounds again with a 16-7 championship win in Yankee Stadium. For 1963 the Chicago Bears, with George Halas as coach, had edged out Green Bay as New York's opponent. The Bears' trademark was their defense, directed by assistant coach George Allen. The Giants, of course, cornered the offensive market, averaging better than 32 points a game with Tittle throwing for more than 3100 yards. He would, however, have trouble de-icing his air attack in Chicago's eight-degree weather.

He tallied early with a 14-yard touchdown pass to Frank Gifford, but injured his left knee when Bear linebacker Larry Morris nailed him on the play. Despite the pain, he returned moments later after a Bears' turnover to fling a bomb to split end Del Shofner in the end zone. Shofner dropped it.

Then Morris added to the insult by intercepting a screen pass to set up the Bears' first touchdown. The Giants later went ahead by a field goal, 10-7, but Morris levelled Tittle again before the half, worsening the torn ligaments. Still, Tittle returned in the third quarter, only to throw an interception that led to the Bears' second score and a 14-10 lead, the winning margin. Twice after that the limping Tittle drove the Giants downfield only to be intercepted each time. The game ended with his fifth interception.

While not victorious, the effort is remembered for its character. Yet for Tittle and the Giants, that held little consolation, because the game was one they could have, should have, won.

Left: Cleveland Browns Jimmy Brown (top) and New York Giants Y A Tittle pose in December 1963 as double winners of the 'Jim Thorpe Memorial Award,' presented annually to the top professional football player of the year.
Above: Tittle is helped off the field during the 1963 NFL title game.
Above right: The Browns' Lou 'The Toe' Groza kicks a field goal during the 1964 NFL Championship game.

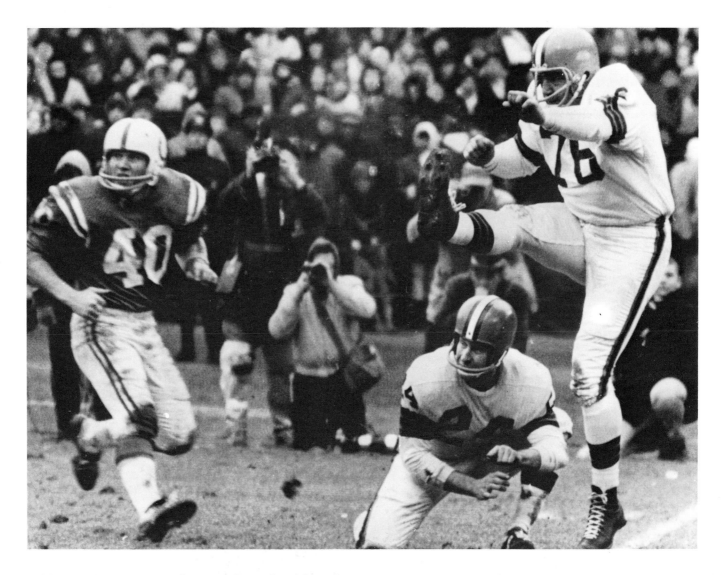

The Baltimore Colts vs. the Cleveland Browns, 27 December 1964

The Baltimore Colts were considered substantial favorites to win the 1964 championship over the Cleveland Browns. In the days leading up to the title game, that forecast wore a bit thin with Cleveland coach Blanton Collier.

The newspapers and pigskin prognosticators figured the Colts' dominant offense would shred a Cleveland defense that had struggled most of the season.

As any good coach would, the mild-mannered Collier allowed the pre-championship snubbing to build the emotional level of his team. But Collier knew that emotion alone wouldn't beat the Colts. To do that, he and his assistants would have to figure out how their slow defensive secondary was going to stop Baltimore's passing whiz, Johnny Unitas.

In studying game films, Collier detected that Unitas shuffled his feet in the pocket toward his primary receiver, which was usually Raymond Berry. The defensive backfield could read that cue, then focus extra effort on momentarily cutting off Unitas from his prime target. That, Collier and his coaches figured, would allow the Browns' pass rush an extra instant to reach the Colts' quarterback.

The home crowd of nearly 80,000 had something to cheer about that afternoon in Cleveland Municipal Stadium. With a mix of man-for-man and zone pass defense, the Browns threw a net over Unitas' options and turned the first half into a scoreless defensive testing ground. The Colts threatened once early, but from there the day belonged to the underdogs.

In the second half, Cleveland's offensive performance caught up with the defense. The Browns' quarterback Frank Ryan ran the Colts' secondary crazy with a 27-point outburst that included three touchdown passes to veteran receiver Gary Collins.

For the day, Ryan threw for 206 yards, completing 11 of 18 passes. Collins caught five passes for 130 yards and the three scores.

Whenever the Baltimore defense focused on the air game, Jim Brown gouged them on the ground.

The Cleveland defense continued to shackle and confuse Unitas throughout the second half, holding him to just 95 yards passing for the game. When it was over, the Browns had added a 27-0 shutout to their stock of championships.

'They took it away from us,' Baltimore coach Don Shula told reporters afterward. 'They were better prepared than we were.'

Collier's comments weren't so important. It was his championship smile that told the story.

Sayers Runs to Immortality, 12 December 1965

As far as pro football careers go, Gale Sayers' was brief but bright. Very bright.

A college star from the University of Kansas, Sayers was the third player selected in the first round of the 1965 pro draft. Chicago's George Halas had scouted him since his freshman year in college, and the Chicago boss held his breath while the New York Giants selected Tucker Frederickson and the San Francisco 49ers took Ken Willard before he could select Sayers.

For all his elation, Halas didn't rush Sayers into the fray. Instead, the Chicago coach held back the young runner in the first two games, allowing him to adjust slowly to the NFL. But after a time, Halas realized there was no way to restrain brilliance. In the fifth game, Sayers led the Bears to a 45-37 victory over the Minnesota Vikings by shifting and feinting his way to four touchdowns. Fans knew it wouldn't be long before Sayers was pushing the single-game touchdown record of six scores shared by Dub Jones and Ernie Nevers.

With Sayers scoring seemingly at will, the Bears ran off eight victories after having lost the season's first three games. Going into the twelfth game against San Francisco, Sayers had scored 16 touchdowns, four short of the NFL season record held by Baltimore's Lenny Moore.

The 49ers had pounded the Bears, 52-24, early in the season, but this was a new Chicago team with Sayers. It didn't take long for the 49ers to find that out. Chicago's Wrigley Field was soggy that December afternoon, but Sayers seemed to glide along the loose turf, cutting and reversing with ease. When it was over, the rookie had scored six touchdowns and amassed 336 all-purpose yards as the Bears returned the favor to San Francisco, 61-20.

'That was the greatest performance I've ever seen on the football field by one man,' Halas told sportswriters afterward.

'If it had been dry, he would have scored ten,' Bear tight end Mike Ditka remarked.

He dazzled the 49ers early with an 80-yard run with a screen pass in which he broke through a crowd of defenders and then sprinted to the goal. He followed that with runs of 21, 7, 50 and 1 yards. Late in the game, he capped a perfect afternoon with an 85-yard punt return. When reporters asked him afterward how he ran so well in the mud, Sayers said, 'Most backs cut on the balls of their feet. But I cut on my heels. That helps me keep my footing in the mud.'

Sayers' star reached its zenith early in a career that would be shortened by knee injuries. Yet it was obvious that in a very short time, Gale Sayers had set a new standard.

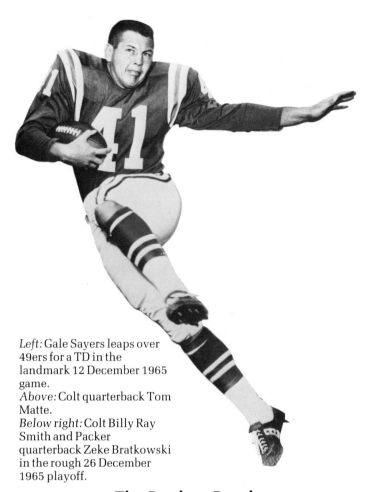

Left: Gale Sayers leaps over 49ers for a TD in the landmark 12 December 1965 game.
Above: Colt quarterback Tom Matte.
Below right: Colt Billy Ray Smith and Packer quarterback Zeke Bratkowski in the rough 26 December 1965 playoff.

The Backup Bowl
Colts vs. Packers, 26 December 1965

It may not have been the greatest game ever played. But the Western Conference playoff between Green Bay and Baltimore in December 1965 was certainly one of the roughest. Actually it was a rough game in a rough season. The close of the regular schedule had left the Colts decimated at quarterback. First, Johnny Unitas fractured his knee in Baltimore's ninth game, then backup Gary Cuozzo separated his shoulder in the eleventh game, a loss.

They were replaced by Tom Matte, a third stringer converted from running back. He had played quarterback in Woody Hayes' run-oriented T-formation at Ohio State. The Colts' coach Don Shula adjusted the offense and even typed up some plays to fit inside Matte's wristband.

Despite the problems with quarterback, Baltimore almost finessed the playoffs. Matte led them to a win in the last game against Los Angeles. Things looked even brighter when he helped them to a 10-0 first half lead in the playoffs the next week against the Packers. But Green Bay drove for a late-game field goal to tie the score at 10, then pushed into position for the winning field goal with more than 13 minutes gone in sudden-death overtime.

The 13-10 victory had a dear price. The Packers' battered casualties included quarterback Bart Starr,

running back Paul Hornung, ends Boyd Dowler and Bill Anderson, and tackles Ron Kostelnik and Henry Jordan. 'This was the roughest game I've ever been in,' a weary Herb Adderly said in the locker room.

When Starr went out with injuries early in the first quarter, the game became a battle of backup quarterbacks. Green Bay's match for Matte was 34-year-old Zeke Bratkowski, who found his stride late in the game and directed the drives for the winning points.

Having pulled to 10-7 early in the third quarter, the Packers stalled again until they caught traction with just over nine minutes left in the game. Alternating running and passing plays, Bratkowski took them down to the Colts' 20. But then Tom Moore dropped a third-down pass with just two minutes left. They had to settle for Don Chandler's 27-yard field goal (which the Colts claimed was wide left) and a 10-10 tie.

In overtime the teams played hot potato, trading four futile possessions until Bratkowski gingerly worked the ball into position for Chandler at the Baltimore 18. This time the 25-yard kick was high caliber, setting up the Packers to claim the title the following week against Cleveland. The playoff finish was special for the veterans, Bratkowski and Chandler. 'We must have been the two most excited old men in the country today,' Chandler joked afterward. Certainly they were the happiest.

Circle the Wagons
Cowboys vs. Redskins, 1966-67

The 1966 Dallas Cowboys were proof that if you had the right people, enough money, and the perfect image, you could accomplish almost anything in pro football. The Dallas franchise was started in 1960, and six struggling years later, the people behind it had rounded up a playoff caliber team. Those early Cowpokes weren't so much good as they were excitin'.

And any red-eyed couch potato who's ever watched B-grade westerns till dawn can tell you that there's no faster way to create excitement than to mix gunslingers and Injuns. That simple formula is at the heart of one of the NFL's prickliest rivalries, Washington vs. Dallas, which flowered like a desert cactus (full of barbs) in the mid-1960s.

The chief Redskin in those days was quarterback Sonny Jurgensen, one of the game's all-time great passers, and his targets were the likes of tight end Jerry Smith and running back Charley Taylor. Like their namesakes, the mid-sixties Redskins didn't win the big war, but earned their reputation ambushing the favorites.

The Cowboys, on the other hand, were led by the guile of quarterback Dandy Don Meredith, a slinger with enough poise to hinge a career on the two-minute drill, then graduate to Lipton Tea and Monday Night Football. The Bullet in the Cowboys' offense was Bob Hayes, otherwise known as the world's fastest human. Meredith's other prime receivers were Lance Rentzel and Pete Gent, who would later author *North Dallas Forty*.

The first memorable matchup occurred 28 November 1965, when Jurgy rallied the Skins from a 21-0 deficit to 31-20. Down 31-27 with less than two minutes to play, Jurgensen juggled timeouts and sideline patterns to give Washington the lead, 34-31. Only problem was, he left a minute on the clock for Dandy Don.

Meredith worked the Pokes into field goal range only to see Danny Villaneuva's kick blocked as time expired. The Cowboys got revenge the following 13 November, after Jurgensen pitched his way to a 30-28 Redskin lead late in the game. This time the golden two minutes were Meredith's, as he directed Dallas to the Skins' 12, where Villaneuva punched up the winning kick, 31-30.

A month later, on 11 December 1966, the landrush pace resumed. With less than two minutes left and the score tied, 31-31, Jurgensen drove his team into scoring range, then bled the clock down, before Charley Gogolak kicked the winning field goal for a final score of 34-31. Meredith evened things up the next October with another late drive – 71 yards in 43 seconds – to nip the Skins, 17-14. The football world needed no better proof that the new West was as wild as the old.

Top: In the memorable Dallas-Washington match-up on 28 November 1965, Cowboy halfback J D Smith goes around right end for 10 yards as Leon Donohue blocks a host of charging Redskins.
Above: The Redskins' coach Otto Graham and quarterback Sonny Jurgensen during practice.
Right: Cowboy quarterback Dan Meredith is helped off the field during the fierce Dallas-Washington contest on 11 December 1966.

Taking All Comers
The 1966 Green Bay Packers

The big battle between the NFL and AFL in the 1960s was waged with checkbooks. The beneficiaries were a few bonus baby rookies – namely Joe Namath with a $400,000 contract, Tommy Nobis with $600,000 and Donnie Anderson with $711,000 – a development that didn't sit well with established NFL stars, most of whom were making far less than $100,000.

Then Al Davis, head coach and general manager of the Oakland Raiders, was named AFL commissioner in 1966. Swiftly, Davis targeted the NFL's low-paid veterans as the AFL's talent pool. Facing a bidding war that threatened to wreck both leagues, the NFL owners realized it was time for a merger.

As a prelude, the two leagues decided to feel each other out in a championship game, dubiously dubbed the Super Bowl. Lamar Hunt, one of the AFL founders, had come up with the name, reportedly after watching his daughter play with a Super Ball.

However, the ball in that first game was anything but super. Not to take anything away from history, but the first Super Bowl, a bit of a mismatch between the Green Bay Packers and the Kansas City Chiefs, was upstaged by the preliminaries of the NFL championship between the Packers and the Cowboys.

The Packers were enjoying the zenith of the greatness Vince Lombardi had brought them, with their names – Bart Starr, Jim Taylor, Max McGee, Carroll Dale, Paul Hornung, Willie Davis, Ray Nitschke, Bowd Dowler – having become imbedded in the American consciousness. The Cowboys were just coming into their own as a franchise, finally lassoing the kind of success Texans had come to expect.

The promise of Tom Landry's first really good team nearly evaporated before 74,152 witnesses in the Cotton Bowl on 1 January 1967, as the Packers scored twice to lead, 14-0, before the Cowboys had run one play. They had earned the first one on a sustained drive, but then Mel Renfro had fumbled the kickoff, Jim Grabowski scooped it up, and the Packers had the gimme touchdown they would need to survive to the championship. Not that Dallas wasn't brilliant after that, with Meredith passing and directing the ground game. The Cowboys' answer was two touchdowns of their own to even things at 14 all before the first quarter ended.

Starr reached Dale with a 51-yard bomb in the second quarter, and Dallas added a field goal by Danny Villaneuva before the half. They pulled closer with another field goal in the third. But then Starr drilled two more touchdown scores to Dowler and McGee. When the Cowboys blocked Don Chandler's conversion after the last touchdown, the Packers led, 34-20. Meredith quickly closed the gap with a 68-yard zinger to tight end Frank Clarke, and all Dallas needed was another chance for a tie game and a shot at overtime.

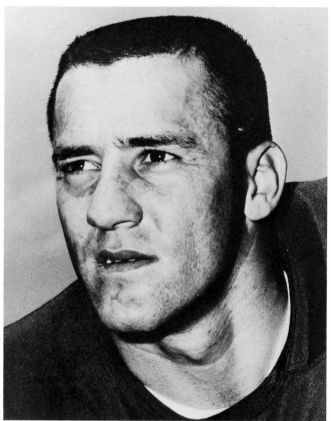

Below left: During the 1967 NFL title game, the Packers' Bart Starr drills a touchdown pass to Boyd Dowler.
Left: Green Bay's Jim Taylor put the Packers ahead to stay with his second-quarter touchdown during the 15 January 1967 Super Bowl against Kansas City.
Above: Packers hold coach Vince Lombardi aloft following their NFL Championship victory over the Cowboys, 1 January 1967.
Far right, below: After receiving a touchdown pass from Starr during the 1 January 1967 championship game, Packer Boyd Dowler is upended in the end zone.
Below: Packer Max McGee sprints for Green Bay's first touchdown of the January 1967 Super Bowl.

They got a second chance, and more, as Meredith drove them to a first down at the Packer two-yard line with time running out. The Packer defenders hunkered down, stopping Dan Reeves for one-yard gain, but on the next play they received help from an unexpected source. Dallas was called for offsides, and the ball was set back at the six. Three straight passes failed, and the Packers were on the way to the first Super Bowl as 13-point favorites.

To everybody's surprise, it was quite a game for a half. Although only 61,946 of the 100,000 seats in Los Angeles Memorial Coliseum were sold, the event had quite an audience – an estimated 60 million combined viewers from NBC and CBS, who shared broadcast rights. A minute of advertising cost $75,000 to $85,000.

Plus there was plenty of outlandish pre-game and halftime entertainment – bands and dancers and batons and such. Somebody had the bright idea of releasing 4000 pigeons just before kickoff.

For a while, the going proved just a bit tougher than the Packers thought it would be. Starr completed a 37-yard touchdown pass to McGee in the first quarter, and Green Bay led, 7-0. Quarterback Len Dawson responded for the Chiefs by finishing off an impressive 66-yard drive with a 7-yard pass to fullback Curtis McClinton. The Packers came back with their own parade, with Jim Taylor rushing 14 yards for a 14-7 lead.

Before the half, the Chiefs added a field goal and took to the locker room the hope that their youth would provide the winning stamina in the second half. The young league certainly had reasons for optimism, but the triumph would come later. The 1967 Super Bowl belonged to the Packers.

Their experience, epitomized by their efficient ground game, prevailed. First, the Packer defense opened the half with a blitz that sacked Dawson three times. Even worse, it forced him to throw an interception to free safety Willie Wood, who returned the ball 50 yards to the Chiefs' five. Elijah Pitts ran the ball over on the next play, and Kansas City's hopes visibly sagged. From there, the Packers controlled the game with two sustained, time-consuming drives for scores. It ended, 35-10.

'I just wish we were in the same conference with Green Bay,' Kansas City's Buck Buchanan said afterward. 'We have people in our league just as good or better. I don't think we got disgraced. We just got beat.'

Buchanan's wish was on its way to becoming true. The outcome was couched in respect, not derision. The first Super Bowl was a good beginning of the healing process between rival leagues.

Cold, Cold Champions
Dallas vs. Green Bay,
31 December 1967

When the Green Bay Packers defeated the Oakland Raiders, 34-14, to win Super Bowl II, the game did little more than confirm that the AFL was still maturing. The real clash in professional football in 1967 came in the preliminary, the NFL championship game, again a gutwrencher between the Cowboys and the Packers. As happened in the 1966 championship, the Cowboys suffered most of the wrenching.

The 1967 game was probably the most frustrating in the short history of the Dallas franchise. Certainly it was the coldest. The game time temperature at Green Bay's Lambeau Field was 13 below zero, with a dastardly windchill factor that played as the Packers' arctic twelfth man. The Packers' coach Vince Lombardi was said to have prayed for a deep cold spell before the game. The answer to those prayers will forever be known as the Ice Bowl.

Green Bay management had installed 14 miles of heater cables six inches beneath the surface of the field to have it warm for the playoffs. But when the temperature dropped rapidly on the eve of the game, the warming system malfunctioned, leaving the damp field to freeze as a slick glass pond. It was a truly miserable day for football, or any outdoor endeavor for that matter. A little more than 50,000 fans suffered through four quarters of chill.

In that setting, the Packers skated to an early 14-0 lead on two Bart Starr touchdown passes. For the Cowboys, the opening was painfully reminiscent of the '66 championship. Things turned momentarily worse when Herb Adderly intercepted a pass and returned it to the Dallas 32 midway through the second period. Facing a rout, the Dallas Doomsday Defense somehow shook off the chill and smothered Green Bay's offense for the rest of the half.

With four minutes left in the second quarter, the Cowboys' Willie Townes hit Starr, forcing a fumble at the Green Bay seven, which George Andrie grabbed up and ran into the end zone for a touchdown. Dallas narrowed the deficit to 14-10 just before the half on a Danny Villanueva field goal.

The scoring was as frozen as the weather until the early moments of the fourth quarter when the Cowboys took a 17-14 lead on a 50-yard halfback option pass from Dan Reeves to Lance Rentzel. The weather Lombardi had prayed for was now lined up against him with the Dallas defense. The combination of the two worked to kill a Don Chandler field goal attempt minutes later. Then Don Meredith and the Dallas offense ran five minutes off the clock before punting to the Green Bay 32. There, with 4:54 on the clock, the Packers jumpstarted their offense. Between them and an unprecedented third NFL championship stood 68 yards, the cold, and one of football's best defenses.

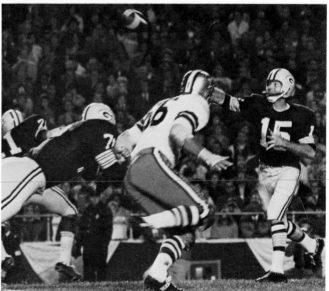

Far left: Packer Herb Adderly helped his team to a 21-17 victory over the Cowboys on 31 December 1967.
Left: Green Bay's stellar quarterback, Bart Starr.
Right: The Cowboys' Lance Rentzel put his team ahead temporarily in the last quarter of the 1967 NFL Championship game, when he scored on a 50-yard pass from Dan Reeves.

Left: Bart Starr passes as George Andrie of the Dallas Cowboys rushes in during the 1967 NFL title game.
Above: Packer coach Vince Lombardi, on the sidelines during the 1967 NFL title game. The Packers beat the Cowboys, 21-17.

Afterward, in the locker room, Packer guard Jerry Kramer recalled the mood in the huddle: 'Maybe this is the year we don't make it, that it all ends. But I know every guy made up his mind that if we were going down, we were going down trying.' In that frame of mind, the Packers started their last-ditch drive. First there was a six-yard gain by running back Donny Anderson. Then reserve running back Chuck Mercein sliced off tackle for a first down. Starr next threw to Bowd Dowler at the Dallas 42. Just as the momentum crested, the Cowboys threw Anderson for a loss, but Starr answered with two quick completions to Anderson for a first down at the 30, with 1:35 left. Mercein then caught a pass and raced to the 11, where he ran out of bounds to stop the clock. On the next play, Mercein dashed off tackle for eight yards to the three.

There, on a plane of ice, the two teams played out one of pro football's classic dramas. Two rushes by Anderson netted two yards and a first down. On third down and goal at the one with 0:016 left, Starr called for a dive between Kramer and center Ken Bowman. But rather than risk a handoff, Starr made the play a keeper.

Said Kramer in the locker room later: 'He was going to go for the hole just inside me, just off my left shoulder. Kenny Bowman and I were supposed to move big Jethro Pugh out of the way. The ground was giving me trouble, the footing was bad down near the goal line, but I dug my cleats in, got a firm hold with my right foot, and we got down into position, and Bart called the "hut" signal. Jethro was on my inside shoulder, my left shoulder. I slammed into Jethro hard, coming off the ball as fast as I ever have in my life. All he had time to do was raise his left arm. He didn't even get it up all the way, and I charged into him. . . . With Bowman's help I moved him outside. . . . Bart churned into the opening and stretched and fell and landed over the goal line.'

The Packers had won their third straight NFL championship, 21-17. The beaming face of Vince Lombardi in the dressing room was broadcast to America: 'This is what the Packers are all about — what we did in the last two minutes,' he told reporters. 'They don't do it for individual glory. They do it because they respect each other and have a feeling for the other fellow.'

The Brilliance of Broadway
The 1968 Jets and Super Bowl III

The 1968 season marked the coming of age of pro football, a mirroring of society at large in the sixties as American youth sought to shirk the rigid conservatism of the past for a colorful new liberalism. The color and excitement of the younger American Football League had been encased in a second class status, dominated by the hard-nosed old guard of the NFL, Vince Lombardi and the Green Bay Packers.

Yet everything that seemed so stable changed quite suddenly in 1968. Without Lombardi (who ceased coaching to become the team's general manager) the Packers stumbled and were replaced by the aging but powerful Baltimore Colts. What followed was nothing less than a sports revolution, if not football's greatest moment, certainly its most entertaining season. It was the dawning of the Age of Aquarius. The moon was in its seventh house; Jupiter was aligned with Mars. And the AFL? Well, its time had come, arrived, so to speak, on the shoulder pads of the New York Jets, led by a young quarterback full of moxie and mouth: Broadway Joe Namath.

There are still those who believed he talked the Jets to the championship, that he assumed the throne without firing a shot, that America, the Baltimore Colts included, bought the grandest of sales pitches. Don't you believe it. From start to finish, the Jets' 1968 season was a victory for team football. That's not to say that Super Joe didn't spice the proceedings with the heaviest public display of individual confidence pro football had ever witnessed. Now that history has had a chance to mull it over, Namath's youthful braggadocio in the days before Super Bowl III seems the perfect narrative for the AFL's tumultous uprising.

It was perhaps pro football's most entertaining year.

First, there was the 'Heidi' game, the network gaffe that infuriated millions of television viewers but ultimately drew more attention to the raging competition in the AFL. Of course, Namath and the Jets were among the central characters, but they shared the lead with Daryle Lamonica and the perpetually dastardly Oakland Raiders. Aired by NBC, the 17 November matchup was a preview of the league championship. It was a darts match between Namath and Lamonica, an exchange of bullseyes featuring 71 passes and 19 penalties. Stretched by the style, the game was much longer than expected, developing into a 29-29 tie in the closing minutes. Then New York added a field goal for a 32-29 lead with a little over a minute left. Within seconds Lamonica pitched the Raiders to the Jets' 43 for a thrilling close.

That's when NBC officials abruptly switched to a scheduled broadcast of 'Heidi,' the children's classic. Only viewers in the West, where it was 4:00 PM, were allowed to see the dramatic climax. Thousands of others in the East were outraged and immediately

Above left: An official signals touchdown as Packer Bart Starr plunges over the line with the score that won the 1967 NFL Championship for Green Bay.
Above: The Oakland Raiders' quarterback Daryle Lamonica led his team to a 43-32 victory over Namath's Jets in the exciting 17 November 1968 match-up.

jammed NBC's switchboards with complaints. NBC President Julian Goodman was among the jilted fans but couldn't get a call through. The network waited more than an hour to flash the outcome across the bottom of the screen: Oakland 43, New York 32. Lamonica had thrown a 43-yard scoring pass to Charlie Smith with 43 seconds left, then the Jets fumbled the kickoff and Preston Ridelhuber picked up the ball and scored again.

That scathing pace resumed 29 December in the AFC Championship, played in the chill, swirling winds of New York's Shea Stadium. Oakland had gotten there by winning the Western Division with a 12-2 record, then eliminating the Kansas City Chiefs 41-6, in a playoff; the Jets had zipped the Eastern with 11 wins and 3 losses. The weather grounded both air attacks early in the championship. But Namath used his favorite receiver, Don Maynard, to work on Oakland's rookie cornerback George Atkinson. Maynard beat Atkinson for a 14-yard touchdown pass in the first quarter, and a short time later, New York added a field goal for a 10-0 lead. Lamonica opened up the Raiders in the second period with a 29-yard scoring pass to Fred Biletnikoff, then Jim Turner's second field goal pushed New York a little farther ahead, 13-7. George Blanda matched that moments later with a Raider field goal, and the Jets led 13-10 at the half.

Another Blanda field goal evened the score at 13 in the third, but Namath pushed the Jets back into the lead with an 80-yard drive and a 20-yard scoring pass to tight end Pete Lammons. After Blanda kicked his third field goal to bring the Raiders within four, Namath resumed his attack on Atkinson. The Oakland corner responded with an interception and return to the New York five, setting up Oakland's go-ahead touchdown. Namath lashed back 30 seconds later with a bomb to Maynard at the Oakland six. On the next play, he threw again to Maynard in the corner of the end zone for a 27-23 Jets' lead.

Lamonica had six minutes left to work some magic. His first effort died when he was sacked at the New York 26 on fourth and 10. The second effort took the Raiders to the Jets' 24, where a fumbled lateral ended Oakland's hopes.

The Jets were headed to the Super Bowl in Miami, but that didn't matter much, according to the pundits. The Baltimore Colts, with 15 wins against a single loss, were 18- to 23-point favorites. Johnny Unitas was slowed by injuries, leaving veteran Earl Morrall as the Colts' quarterback, but that seemed to make little difference as Baltimore humiliated Cleveland, 34-0, in the NFL Championship. The Baltimore defense was the real foundation of the squad, and just about everyone figured it would make mincemeat of Super Joe and company – which made Namath's mouthing off to the press in the days before the Super Bowl seem all the more preposterous. 'The Jets will win on Sunday,' he told the Miami Touchdown Club three days before the game. 'I guarantee it.' Later he told reporters that Morrall wasn't as good as three or four AFL quarterbacks. Then he was reported to have told the Colts' defensive end Lou Michaels, 'We're going to beat the hell out of you.' The Colts were a little taken aback by the woofing. 'All this Namath talk isn't going to fire us up,' grumbled Baltimore's Bubba Smith.

The game had additional subplots. Weeb Ewbank, the New York coach, had directed Baltimore to world championships in 1958 and 1959, only to be

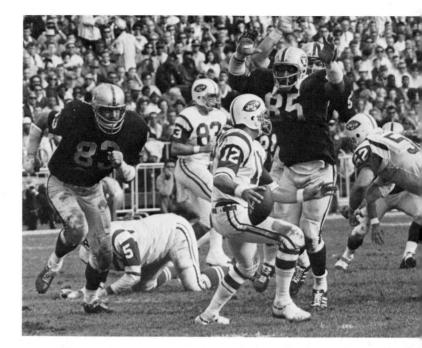

Top: Jets quarterback Joe Namath is dwarfed by the Raiders' massive linemen during the 17 November 1968 game.
Above: Raider rookie Charlie Smith scores from three yards out after getting a good block from Jim Harvey in the third quarter of the Heidi game.

Right: Leaping high to break up a pass to Willie Richardson, Jets Johnny Sample demonstrates how his team's secondary picked apart the Colts' passing game throughout the 12 January 1969 Super Bowl.
Far right: Jets coach Weeb Ewbank is congratulated by defensive back Mike D'Amato (47) and end Bake Turner as they leave the field victorious after Super Bowl III.

let go after a .500 season in 1962. And Johnny Sample, firebrand in the Jets' secondary, had been traded by the Colts after their championships.

And, in a more restrained snobbish manner, the Colts matched Namath's talk with haughtiness. Club and network (NBC had paid $2.5 million for broadcast rights) officials began planning the victory celebration in the Baltimore locker room. The Colts' owner Carroll Rosenbloom went so far as to invite Ewbank to his victory party. The Colts, it's fair to say, played as they acted: fatly overconfident. Still, they were presented ample opportunity in the first half to make the game a blowout. It just wasn't in the stars.

The Jets received and immediately established a ground game, with Matt Snell running effectively into the face of the Baltimore defense. The drive died after four minutes but it built New York's confidence. After a punt, the Colts promptly shoved their way down the field to a first down at the Jets' 19, where a pass was dropped and Michaels missed a 27-yard field goal. Moments later, George Sauer Jr fumbled on New York's 12, and the Colts had another chance. Jet defensive back Randy Beverly intercepted a Morrall pass in the end zone.

The Baltimore defense was successful in shutting down Namath's primary target, Maynard, so he threw to Sauer instead, moving the Jets on an impressive drive to the Baltimore four, where Snell ran the ball in for a 7-0 lead. Again, the Colts forged back, taking the ball to the Jets' 16 on the strength of a 58-yard run by Tom Matte. Again, the Jets prevailed, this time with Sample getting the interception in the end zone.

Still, the Colts returned to scoring position yet a fourth time just before the half, but Morrall failed to see wide-open Jimmy Orr at the Jets' 10. Instead he threw to the other side of the field and suffered a third interception.

The second half opened with Unitas eager to play, but the Colts' coach Don Shula started Morrall again. Then Matte fumbled on the opening play, New York recovered and increased the lead to 10-0 on a Jim Turner field goal. After Morrall failed to move the team a second time, Shula inserted Unitas. But the Jets had shut down Baltimore's strong ground game and defended the pass ferociously. Meanwhile, Namath was troubled by a thumb injury and replaced by backup veteran Babe Parilli, who took the Jets to another third quarter field goal and a 13-0 lead.

When Turner kicked yet another field goal two minutes into the fourth quarter for a 16-0 lead, the task for Baltimore became nearly impossible. With four minutes left, Jerry Hill scored on a one-yard dive and the NFL's dominant team avoided a shutout.

In the locker room, the Jets had fun pointing out the absence of a fluke. The game was won, they said, on complete efforts by the secondary, the offensive line, the defensive line – everybody. 'We didn't win on passing or running or defense,' said MVP Namath, who had completed 17 of 28 passes for 208 yards. 'We beat 'em in every phase of the game. If ever there was a world champion, this is it.'

For the AFL, for all of football, it was a triumph of style.

THE SEVENTIES

Dempsey's Great Kick 8 November 1970

That Tom Dempsey kicked at all was amazing. That he kicked an NFL record 63-yard field goal, winning a game for the New Orleans Saints in the process, was seemingly impossible. Just don't tell Tom Dempsey that. He was born with only half a kicking foot and only two fingers on his right hand.

But he was blessed with a father who took an interest in him, who worked with him to overcome the birth defect. As a result, what could have been a debilitating handicap was nothing more than an oddity. He played offensive and defensive football in high school and at Palomar Junior College, but his real development was as a kicker.

His foot, flattened by nature into a stub with no toes, was suited for kicking. But Dempsey had to work to make it the lethal weapon it became. He received attention from the pros while playing semipro ball in the Atlantic Coast Football League, and in 1968 he earned a spot on the roster of the San Diego Chargers, where his specially designed kicking shoe, flat across the front, quickly became an item of curiosity.

He rapidly gained a reputation as a proud player, quick to reject unwanted sympathy, eager to display his toughness. He was not always the best at following training rules, although no one questioned his dedication to the game. And he wasn't immune to dreadful kicking slumps. In fact, he had just begun working his way out of one in the fall of 1970 when he found his niche in history. He had been picked up by the Saints after being placed on waivers by San Diego, and was their primary offensive weapon on 8 November in a game against the Detroit Lions. Dempsey had kicked three field goals to keep the Saints in a nip-and-tuck race with the Lions.

But with just 13 seconds left, the Lions' Errol Mann had punched up an 18-yard field goal to give Detroit a 17-16 lead. A good kickoff return and a quick completion left the Saints at their own 45 with two seconds left. Coach J D Roberts was left with the choice of a desperation pass or Dempsey for a 63-yard field goal attempt.

Dempsey was confident of the range, not the accuracy. Most of the Lions' defensive front thought the effort a joke. But the chuckling stopped when holder Joe Scarpati put down the placement, and Dempsey hit the ball solidly.

He knew it was good.

Left: New Orleans Saints kicker Tom Dempsey watches one of his kicks split the uprights for a first half score against the Lions on 8 November 1970. Dempsey kicked four field goals in that game, the final kick a record 63 yards, with two seconds left, to give the Saints a 19-17 win.

Right, above: The Oakland Raiders' kicker and backup quarterback, 43-year-old George Blanda, was voted the AFC's Most Valuable Player in 1970.
Right: George Blanda watches the game from the sidelines.

Ageless George Blanda
Fall 1970

George Blanda earned a name as the old man of pro football, with a playing career that spanned some part of the four decades. For a while, it seemed the older he got, the better he played. At least Oakland fans believed that in the fall of 1970, when Blanda worked come-from-behind miracles on five successive weekends. All that from a spring chicken of 43.

Blanda first entered the NFL in 1949, when Harry Truman was president, and he retired in 1975, when Gerald Ford was taking over the White House. After 11 uneventful seasons, the Bears released him in 1959, at age 31, just in time for the birth of the new-fangled AFL. Blanda was only happy to catch on with the Houston Oilers, where he became a star quarterback and kicker, leading his team to three championship games. Then in 1967, figuring time had caught up with the 37-year-old Blanda, the Oilers also released him. In 1968 the Oakland Raiders saw Blanda's worth and picked him up as a kicker and backup quarterback. The game, however, has little respect for its elders, and just before the 1970 season, Blanda was again placed on waivers. When the Raiders could find no one better in training camp, they reclaimed him, setting the stage for one of the league's all-time individual performances.

Oakland began uncertainly in 1970, with a 2-2-1 record after five games. Then first-string quarterback Daryle Lamonica was injured early in pivotal game six against the Pittsburgh Steelers with the score tied at 7. Blanda came in and threw three touchdown passes for a 31-14 Raider win. The next week Lamonica returned, but with three seconds left, Oakland trailed Kansas City, 17-14. Blanda confidently kicked a 48-yard field goal for a tie. Cleveland came to the Bay area after that and held a 17-13 lead in the fourth quarter when Lamonica was again injured. Blanda's first pass was intercepted, setting up a Browns' field goal and a 20-13 lead. Given a second chance, he drove his team to a tying touchdown, then worked

them into field goal range minutes later with only three seconds left. From the Cleveland 45, he kicked a 52-yarder for a 23-20 win.

As the Oakland crowd erupted, the Raiders' play-by-play radio man Bill King shouted, 'I don't believe it . . . George Blanda has just been elected king of the world.' Soon after, of course, the fan mail and good wishes poured in.

Blanda answered with another miracle the following week. Down 19-17 to the Denver Broncos with four minutes left, the Raider coaches decided to insert Blanda for a last drive. He took the team 80 yards and won the game with a 20-yard TD pass to Fred Biletnikoff.

The cap on the streak came the next week against San Diego, where with seven seconds left, Blanda beat the Chargers, 20-17, with a 16-yard field goal. The Raiders won the divisional championship on the momentum of his magic.

Blanda's reaction to the hoopla? Low key and unassuming. Yet he didn't deny his satisfaction at the end of the season when he was voted the AFC's Most Valuable Player. Not bad for an old man.

The Longest Game
Miami vs. Kansas City, Christmas 1971

The Christmas Day 1971 AFC playoff between the Miami Dolphins and Kansas City Chiefs had it all. A kicking duel pitting Miami's Garo Yepremian against KC's Jan Stenerud. The all-star performance of the Chief's Ed Podolak. The fearsome defense of Kansas City linebacker Willie Lanier. The passing of Len Dawson and Bob Griese. The inside/outside of Miami's Jim Kiick and Larry Csonka. A photo finish. All of it wrapped in six periods of play, two sudden-death overtimes. With 82 minutes, 40 seconds of regulation action, it was the longest game in NFL history.

The Dolphins had never beaten Kansas City in the previous six games the two teams had played. Both had finished with 10-3 records, but it appeared that Kansas City was headed for a seventh straight victory when the Chiefs scored 10 quick points. The Dolphins scored the same number in the second quarter, and the second half became a touchdown barter session, with each team trading two.

The memorable performance came from Podolak, who totalled 350 all-purpose yards – 100 rushing, 100 receiving and 150 returning kicks. But in the end, the game was decided by placekickers. The night before the game, Stenerud was named to represent the AFC in the Pro Bowl, a slight to Yepremian, who had led the conference in scoring.

Right: Miami's quarterback Bob Griese prepares to throw. *Below:* The Dolphins' Garo Yepremian, whose field goal decided the longest game on Christmas 1971, was the AFC's scoring and field goal leader that year.

Stenerud had a chance to win the game with seconds left in regulation, but missed from the 31-yard line. He got a second try in the first overtime, from 42 yards out, but Miami linebacker Nick Buoniconti broke through the line and snuffed it. When Yepremian missed from 52 yards, the game slipped into its second overtime. Weariness became the primary factor, but Csonka drew on his reserves for a 29-yard run to set up Yepremian's 37-yard game winner. Given his choice, Yepremian decided he'd take the Super Bowl over the Pro Bowl any day.

Above: Surrounded by Raiders, Pittsburgh's Franco Harris runs downfield. Harris' 'immaculate reception' won the 1972 AFC divisional playoff for his Steelers.
Right: Steeler quarterback Terry Bradshaw threw the ball, intended for John Fugua, that Harris caught to defeat Oakland in the December 1972 playoff game.

Last Minute Magic
23 December 1972

Without question, 23 December 1972 was one of the NFL's strangest days. Depending on the perspective, it was an afternoon of absolutes – delight or disaster. The NFL playoffs offer no middle ground. For Californians, who are supposedly used to weird occurrences, there was no consolation as both Bay area teams – Oakland and San Francisco – lost with last-minute reversals. For Dallas and Pittsburgh, the beneficiaries, the fourth quarter was laced with luck. The Steelers, in particular, considered the outcome immaculate.

In Pittsburgh's Three Rivers Stadium, the first three and a half quarters of the AFC divisional playoff game between the Steelers and the Raiders were hardly memorable. The first half was scoreless, then Pittsburgh struggled to the lead with two Roy Gerela field goals in the third and fourth quarters. Shortly thereafter a young Oakland quarterback named Ken Stabler replaced Daryle Lamonica on the Raiders' last-ditch drive. With 1:13 left, Stabler, who would come to be known by the nickname 'Snake,' scampered 30 yards for a touchdown and a 7-6 Oakland lead.

It was only the second touchdown allowed by the Steelers over five games, but it appeared to be enough to beat them. With 22 seconds left, they faced a fourth and 10 at their own 40. Quarterback Terry Bradshaw dropped into the pocket to pass, realized he faced heavy pressure and scrambled right, where he stopped and blazed the ball over the middle to running back John 'Frenchy' Fuqua, who was covered by Oakland safety Jack Tatum.

Whether physics or fate took over next is the question still debated in Oakland. The ball, Fuqua and Tatum came together at the 35. The two players fell, but the ball ricocheted toward Pittsburgh running back Franco Harris, who was trailing the play. Harris nabbed the ball at his ankles and raced to the end zone, where the arguments began.

Oakland players claimed the ball had hit Fuqua and bounced into Harris. The rules in those days said such a carom from one offensive player to another was an incomplete pass. The Steelers, on the other hand, argued that the ball had hit Tatum. The field referees consulted with the supervisor of officials in the press box and declared the play a touchdown, leaving the Raiders cursing amid the din of celebration at Three Rivers.

Myron Copeland, the Steelers' radio man, dubbed the play, the 'Immaculate Reception.' The Raiders simply called it bad officiating. Fuqua, for his part, grinned and said he was remaining mum.

Three hours later, the San Francisco 49ers suffered a similar late-game disappointment. But they had nobody to blame but themselves. The outcome was an all-too-painful reminder of the 49ers' late-game failure in the 1957 playoffs, when they blew a 24-7 halftime lead and lost to Detroit, 31-27. Despite the ending, the game certainly started well, when San Francisco's Vic Washington ran the opening kickoff back 97 yards for a touchdown. Dallas answered with a field goal, but the 49ers turned Cowboy turnovers into two more touchdowns and a 21-3 lead.

Dallas quarterback Craig Morton finally reversed things just before the half, driving the Cowboys to a field goal and a touchdown to narrow the gap to 21-13.

Roger Staubach had spent most of the year on the bench with a separated shoulder, but Cowboy coach Tom Landry decided to play him after the 49ers scored a third quarter touchdown to take a 28-13 lead. Staubach promptly fumbled, providing San Francisco with a fifth turnover. The ensuing field goal miss by Bruce Gossett was the difference in the game.

From that point on, Staubach ignited a scoring explosion. First, he drove Dallas to a field goal, to pull to 28-16. Then, with 2:02 left in the game, he started another drive. Only 32 seconds and 55 yards later, he hit Billy Parks with a 20-yard touchdown pass. With 90 seconds left, the 49ers led, 28-23, but San Francisco fans had good cause for queasiness.

The Cowboys tried an onsides kick, 49er Preston

Above left: Diagram depicts the freakish Bradshaw-Harris play that ushered Pittsburgh into the 1972 AFC Championship game.
Above: Steeler Franco Harris is mobbed by fans at Three Rivers Stadium after scoring the winning touchdown against the Raiders on 23 December 1972.
Right: Cowboy quarterback Roger Staubach came into the 24 December 1972 playoff game in the third quarter and brought his team from behind to defeat the 49ers, 30-28.

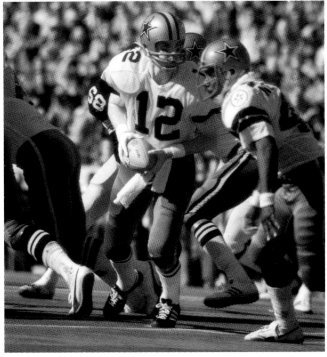

Riley seemed to pull it in, but Dallas rookie Ralph Coleman slammed into him, and Mel Renfro covered the loose ball. Staubach was incredibly efficient. He scrambled for 21 yards, then passed to Parks for another 19. When San Francisco blitzed on the next play, he zipped the go-ahead TD pass to Ron Sellers. The Cowboys led, 30-28. Only a perfectionist would complain that he left 52 seconds on the clock for 49er quarterback John Brodie to go to work. With three quick passes, San Francisco moved to the Dallas 22, only to have the drive stalled by a holding penalty.

The game – and one of football's strangest days – ended with a Brodie interception. Nothing immaculate for the Cowboys. Just a nice piece of work.

Perfection
The 1972 Miami Dolphins

As far as greatest moments go, the 1972 Miami Dolphins made theirs last for a season. Coached by Don Shula, fortified by the 'No Name Defense,' and powered in the backfield by Larry Csonka, Mercury Morris and Jim Kiick, the Dolphins finished a perfect 17-0 season on 14 January 1973 with a 14-7 win over the Washington Redskins in Super Bowl VII. To quote a popular beer commercial, it doesn't get any better than that. Never before, and never since, has any NFL team completed an unbeaten season.

It was only fitting that Don Shula, a fretful perfectionist, should be the coach to achieve perfection. Perhaps more than the unbeaten record, the game was important for the demons it exorcised from Shula's memory. He had been the coach of the heavily favored Baltimore Colts when they were trimmed by Joe Namath and the New York Jets in 1969. The outcome had left difficult feelings between Shula and Colts' owner Carroll Rosenbloom. So in 1970, Shula moved to the Miami Dolphins' struggling young franchise. A year later, he had guided them to a 12-3-1 record and an appearance in Super Bowl VI opposite the Dallas Cowboys. There, Shula became the first coach to lose two Super Bowls.

The Miami Dolphins began training camp that next summer with a whirlwind of intensity. The high pressure system creating it was Don Shula's considerable pride. He wanted nothing less than absolute victory. The storm gathered on opening day and started with a fury, levelling Kansas City and Houston before reaching a brief lull against Minnesota. After a narrow 16-14 win over the Vikings, the Dolphins blew past the New York Jets and San Diego, then paused to struggle with Buffalo. Again, Shula's intensity was the driving force behind a 24-23 victory. Three games and three victories later, Bob Griese, Shula's excellent quarterback, broke an ankle and had to be replaced by 38-year-old Earl Morrall.

The storm seemed to have dissipated to a squall, but with Morrall leading, Miami resumed its pace, slicing through nine straight opponents to finish the regular season, 14-0. That was followed by decisive playoff wins over Cleveland and Pittsburgh, setting up a Super Bowl confrontation between Miami and George Allen's Washington Redskins.

It had been a nonpareil season. Csonka had

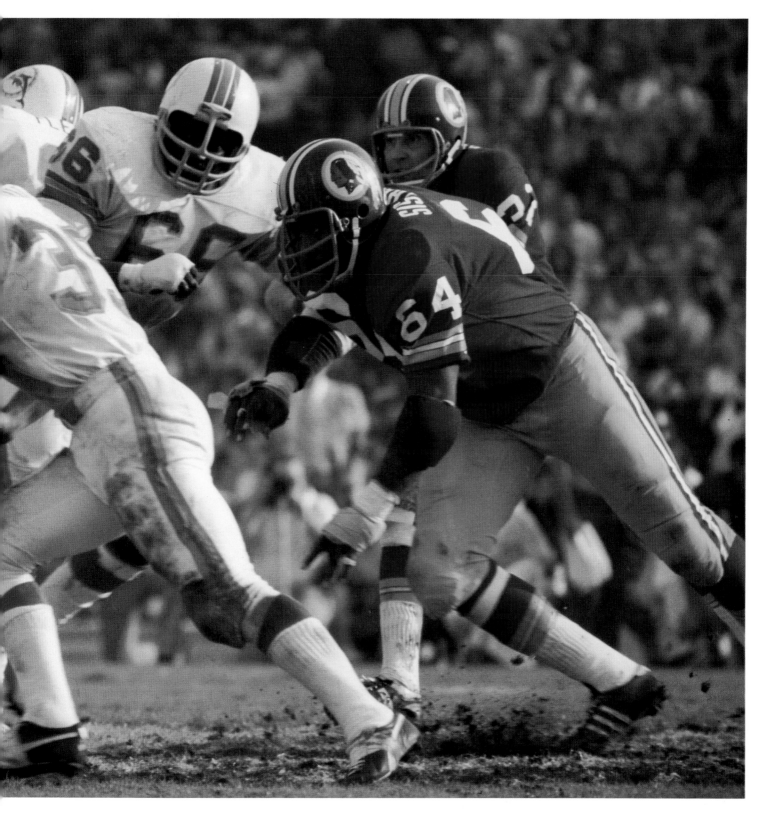

gained 1117 yards, Morris 1000. The Dolphins had outscored their regular season opponents 426 to 202. But that mattered little to Shula. A loss in the Super Bowl would only make them losers again. He wanted nothing short of complete victory. As if the silent anxiety weren't enough, Rosenbloom, new owner of the Los Angeles Rams, commented to the press that Shula would choke in the big game.

Top left: Eugene 'Mercury' Morris, Miami's 1000-yard rusher in 1972, bulls downfield with the ball during Super Bowl VII. *Above:* Miami's Larry Csonka ground out 112 yards for the Dolphins on 15 carries during Super Bowl VII. Miami defeated Washington, 14-7.

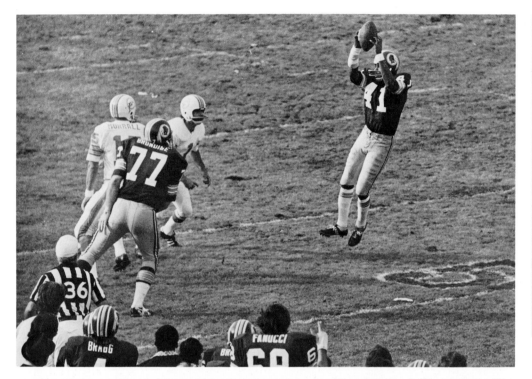

Above left and *Left:* Sequence shots depict the exciting play during Super Bowl VII in which Redskins Mike Bass (41) catches the ball deflected after a Miami field goal attempt and runs it back 49 yards for a touchdown.
Above: The Redskins' head coach George Allen cheers his team on during Super Bowl VII.

Above right: The Buffalo Bills' rushing phenomenon, O J Simpson.
Right: O J Simpson powers his way through the Jets' defense.

The oddsmakers must have believed him, for Allen's 'Over The Hill Gang,' led by Billy Kilmer, was named a three-point favorite. Washington had finished the regular season 11-3, then added playoff victories over Green Bay and Dallas. Both teams relied on the ground game. The tomahawk in the Redskin armory was Larry Brown, who had rushed for 1286 yards in 285 carries. If opponents played the run too closely, Kilmer threw his floating butterball passes to receivers Charley Taylor, Jerry Smith and Roy Jefferson.

Griese had come back from his injury to guide the team to a late touchdown for the win over Pittsburgh,

and Shula tabbed him as the starter in the Super Bowl.

The game, played before 90,000 at Memorial Coliseum in Los Angeles, was controlled by Miami's efficiency. After an early exchange of possessions, the No Name Defense – led by Manny Fernandez, Nick Buoniconti and Jake Scott – pinned the Redskins in their own territory. Miami scored in each of the first two quarters, allowed a second half score off a recovery of Garo Yepremian's fumble, then settled in for a dominating 14-7 victory.

For the fans, for the press, there was no doubt that the Dolphins were the best team in football. As for Shula, his doubt was finally gone, too.

Juiced for the Record
O J Simpson's Rushing Record,
16 December 1973

Orenthel James Simpson earned his reputation at the University of Southern California in 1967 and 1968. When sportswriters reached for metaphor to describe his running style, they settled on ballet. Sure enough, Simpson danced and pirouetted his way to the Heisman trophy, cutting a path that seemed destined for Broadway.

Instead, he opened his NFL show in Buffalo. The Bills, having suffered through a 1-12-1 season, held the first round draft choice in 1968. OJ was the prize. Virtual anonymity was the result. The Bills had little punch on the offensive line, which was nicknamed 'The Vanishing Five.' In his first three professional seasons, Simpson took a beating, rushing for ony 697, 488 and 742 yards respectively.

His thoughts ran to quitting, or seeking to be traded. Then Buffalo hired old hand Lou Saban as coach, and he promptly announced that the offense would center on the Juice. Although the offensive line was decimated by injuries the next season, Simpson still gained 1251 yards on 292 carries, enough to rekindle the Juice's dreams of greatness.

The following year in training camp, he confided to guard Reggie McKenzie, the stalwart on the offensive line, that he thought improved blocking would allow him to rush for 1700 yards. Why not aim for 2000? McKenzie suggested.

Such a journey would take Simpson past a major milepost: Jim Brown's single-season rushing record of 1863 yards. Why not, Simpson decided.

The pace was set the first game against New England, when he rushed for a single-game record 250 yards. By mid-season, he had 1025, and speculation of a 2000-yard season started to build. In game 13, New England was again the foe, and yardage was available. The Juice gained 219 yards on 22 carries. By game 14, the last regular season contest, against the New York Jets, Simpson needed 60 yards to pass Brown and 197 for 2000. The Bills also held slim hopes of a playoff berth (which would later die when Cincinnati beat Houston).

The Bills' first offensive series featured Simpson's 30-yard run and started them on the way to a

Above: O J Simpson's flying feet carry him to still another 200-yard performance on 16 December 1973, for a record-breaking season total of 2003 yards.
Far right: The Raiders' quarterback Kenny 'Snake' Stabler and coach John Madden.
Right: The Dolphins' quarterback Bob Griese calls the signals during the 21 December 1974 playoff against the Raiders.
Above right: The Raiders' end Clifford Branch's 72-yard reception and touchdown put Oakland ahead in the December 1974 playoff against Miami.

commanding lead. He began the next series just four yards short of Brown's record and broke it on the first play, a six-yard sweep. By half, the Bills led 21-7, and the game's competition shifted, from team vs. team to runner vs. real estate. After a 25-yard gain in the third period, he needed less than 50 yards to reach 2000.

The next series was the historic one. Simpson made runs of 8, 22, 9 and 5 yards, bringing him to 1996. Reggie McKenzie led the next play, a gain of 7, that carried Simpson farther than any human had ever gone. After the game, Simpson gathered his offensive line in the spotlight with him. More than a decade later, the Los Angeles Rams' Eric Dickerson would rush for 2105 in 16 games, and Herschel Walker would even better that in the United States Football League's 18-game schedule.

But Juice's per-game total remains the standard, unmatched. Not bad for a billing in Buffalo.

The Big Thrill
Oakland vs. Miami, 21 December 1974

It was a collision of two great teams, both seemingly Super Bowl bound. The Miami Dolphins had appeared in the last three Super Bowls and finished the 1974 race atop the American Conference's Eastern Division. The Raiders had won the Western with a 12-2 record. A network PR man pulled a slick one and billed it 'the real Super Bowl.'

Justified, perhaps, although neither team eventually made it. It could be argued that both reached the zenith of competition that afternoon in Oakland-Alameda County Coliseum. Both Don Shula and John Madden had full houses, the Dolphins featuring Bob Griese at quarterback, Nat Moore and Paul Warfield at receiver, Larry Csonka in the backfield; the Raiders showed Kenny 'Snake' Stabler throwing to Fred Biletnikoff and Cliff Branch.

Moore, in his rookie season, ignited the proceedings by returning the opening kickoff 89 yards for a touchdown. The Raiders couldn't answer until the second quarter when Stabler tied the game with a 31-yard TD toss to Charlie Smith.

It was a margin of noses after that. Garo Yepremian kicked a field goal to give Miami the 10-7 lead at half. Stabler threw to Biletnikoff in the third to make it 14-10. Griese struck back to Warfield, but Yepremian's conversion was blocked by Bubba Smith, 16-14, Miami. Three minutes into the fourth, Yepre-

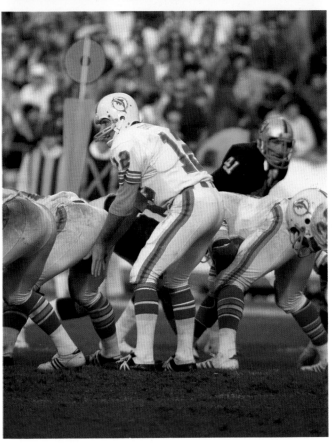

mian's 46-yarder stretched it to 19-14. Then with just under five minutes left, Stabler bombed them with a 72-yarder to Branch, to make it 21-19, Oakland.

By the two and a half minute mark, Griese had returned the Dolphins to the Oakland 23. The Raiders were caught napping with Benny Malone's 23-yard run up the middle. The score now stood at 26-21, Miami.

Shula knew the 2:08 left on the clock was too much. Stabler confirmed it with two quick passes to Biletnikoff, then two more to Branch and Frank Pitts. Clarence Davis then knifed inside to the Miami eight. Just 35 seconds remained. Snake burned his last time out, talked things over with Madden and receiver coach Tom Flores, then attempted a flare pass. The receivers were covered, he scrambled, and just as Dolphins' defensive end Vern Den Herder pulled him down, Stabler cut loose with a desperate dead duck to Clarence Davis in the end zone.

Davis and Miami linebacker Mike Kolen wrestled for the ball. Davis won and assured himself a piece of eternity in an NFL highlight film. Super Bowls could only wish for such drama.

Hail Mary

The Minnesota Vikings were a veteran, balanced team in 1975, and were eager to return to the Super Bowl after having lost pro football's big game the two previous years. Their first obstacle in the playoffs was a young Dallas wild card team, laced with rookies and carrying a 10-4 record into the game at Metropolitan Stadium in Minneapolis.

A cynic would have said that the up-and-down Cowboys didn't have a prayer. The day, of course, would prove differently. The Cowboys, in fact, had several prayers. Their late-game miracle would provide the NFL with an Ave Maria for posterity.

The Vikings recovered a fumbled punt in the second quarter and used the field position to take a 7-0 halftime lead. Dallas evened things up with a third-quarter drive, then took the lead on a Toni Fritsch field goal just minutes into the fourth quarter. Facing the challenge of the season, Fran Tarkenton pulled the Vikings together for a 70-yard drive in 11 plays. Brent McClanahan powered in from the one to make the game 14-10, Minnesota.

Left: Raider quarterback Ken Stabler passes for a gain during the 21 December 1974 game.
Above: Cowboy receiver Drew Pearson makes his way through a sea of blue in the 1975 NFC semi-final playoff game against Minnesota.
Below: Drew Pearson runs the ball downfield.

Faced with a similar challenge, the Cowboy offense fizzled and punted with about three minutes left. The answer would lie with the defense, which had been bolstered with a crop of rookies – Randy White, Herb Scott, Bob Breunig, Thomas Henderson. The telling moment came as Minnesota faced a third and two at the Cowboy 47. Tarkenton eschewed the dive for a rollout. Dallas safety Charlie Waters blitzed and dropped him for a three-yard loss. Reluctantly, the Vikings punted.

The Dallas offense again fizzled. The last hope hinged on a fourth and 16 situation at their own 25. Roger Staubach and receiver Drew Pearson decided to fake a post pattern and angle for the sideline. The momentum of the pass probably would have carried Pearson out of bounds for an incompletion. But he was bumped by cornerback Nate Wright, and the official ruled Pearson had been forced out of bounds.

With 37 seconds left, Dallas had a first down at the 50. When the next pass fell incomplete, Pearson said it was time to work on Wright long again. The pass was short, bringing Pearson back from the end zone to catch it. As he moved to the ball, Wright fell, or as the Vikings claimed, he was knocked down by offensive interference. Pearson caught the ball at the five, clutched it to his waist, then felt it slipping away as he fell into the end zone. With the ball pinned awkwardly at his hip, Pearson glanced around for penalty flags.

There was none, only the dead silence of Metropolitan Stadium. The play became enshrined as 'Hail Mary,' and has become over the years one of the game's hallowed moments.

The Pittsburgh Power
Super Bowl X, 18 January 1976

Receiver Lynn Swann was a wisp of gentility amidst the Pittsburgh Steelers' brutality. Or at least that was his image – an image, of course, that began with his name: Lynn Swann.

W B Yeats couldn't have come up with anything more poetic. The sportswriters immediately reached for descriptions of grace and splendor. Swann surely was all of those things. He could run, he could leap, he could catch, all with a style to match his name. Yet it was his toughness that brought him the MVP Award of Super Bowl X, a toughness that matched his gritty teammates.

The Steelers won four Super Bowls between 1974 and 1980, and to say they did it in 'blue-collar' fashion would be more than a bit trite. Yet there's hardly a way around it. In the age of America's great industrial decline, the Steelers were a lingering symbol of potency. They were hard, polished Pittsburgh steel, running roughshod over the competition with a defense led by Mean Joe Greene, Jack Lambert, L C Greenwood, Jack Ham and Mel Blount. The offense had a similar cast with running backs Rocky Bleier and Franco Harris and quarterback Terry Bradshaw.

Right: Pittsburgh's defenseman Mean Joe Greene, rough and ready.
Below: The Steelers' Lynn Swann, who caught four passes for 161 yards, won the MVP Award of Super Bowl X.

Swann was a mere rookie when the Steelers used their defensive viciousness to subdue the Minnesota Vikings, 16-6, in Super Bowl IX. By the next season, Swann had matured into one of the game's truly gifted pass catchers. Teamed with John Stallworth, he opened up the Steeler offense and helped lead the team to a consecutive Super Bowl appearance.

Along the way, Swann collected his share of bruises, particularly in the AFC title game, a slugfest with the Oakland Raiders. The Steelers won, 16-10, but in the third period Swann collapsed after being nailed by Raider safety George Atkinson. Doctors diagnosed a concussion and kept Swann for observation. Immediately, questions were raised about Swann's ability to play against the Dallas Cowboys in the Super Bowl two weeks away.

Yet within a week, Swann had returned to a limited participation in practice. As it became more apparent he would play in the Super Bowl, the Cowboys began speculating on his effectiveness. Would the head injury make him gun shy? Swann admitted some doubt. 'I thought about it,' he told reporters before the game. 'But finally I said the heck with it. I'm going out there and playing 100 percent.'

Still, all the lingering uncertainty wasn't removed until well into the first quarter at Miami's Orange Bowl. The Cowboys had used Roger Staubach and their shotgun offense to blast to a 7-0 lead. Then Swann stoked the Steelers' first scoring drive with a leaping, acrobatic catch of a Bradshaw pass at the Dallas 16. Somehow, he had retrieved the ball in midair from sailing incomplete out of bounds, then he twisted to land inbounds. Good for 32 yards, the play set up a scoring pass to tight end Randy Grossman moments later.

The teams traded an odd collection of field goals and a safety thereafter until midway into the final quarter. Holding a 15-10 lead at their own 36, Bradshaw and Swann opted for the bomb. Swann set sail, and Bradshaw lofted a fat one for him to run under. The result was another elegant passage in Swann's highlight poem: a 64-yard gamebuster for a 21-10 lead. On the down side, Bradshaw was knocked silly by the Dallas rush and lost for the rest of the game.

Staubach brought the Cowboys right back with a quick touchdown pass, then got the ball back again, trailing 21-17. But the Steel Curtain defense closed out the Dallas performance by intercepting Staubach's final Hail Mary attempt.

The MVP trophy belonged to Swann, who had caught four passes for 161 yards. Not a bad day's work for a blue collar bird.

More Double Trouble Oakland vs. Baltimore, 24 December 1977

The Christmas Eve 1977 AFC Divisional Playoff between the Oakland Raiders and Baltimore Colts was one for the thrill junkies. It had just about all the ingredients for a heart attack, everything from double sudden-death overtime to a ghost and a snake for central characters.

And, as fate would have it, the central characters belonged to the Oakland Raiders – Kenny 'Snake' Stabler at quarterback and Dave 'Ghost' Casper at tight end. Casper caught only four passes in the bullet-riddled afternoon, but three of them were for touchdowns, including the 10-yard winner in the sixth period of play.

Far left: Pittsburgh's running back Franco Harris is downed in Super Bowl X.
Left: Raiders quarterback Ken Stabler fades back to pass. Stabler guided his team to an overtime victory over the Colts in the 1977 AFC divisional playoff.
Below: Raiders tight end Dave 'Ghost' Casper caught three touchdown passes on 24 December 1977.

By any standards the game had a wild pace, with the teams matching big play for big play. Oakland running back Clarence Davis opened the scoring late in the first quarter with a 30-yard touchdown run. Baltimore strong safety Bruce Laird countered in the second with a 61-yard interception return to tie the game, then the Colts took a 10-7 lead just before half.

The third period was just minutes old when Casper caught the first of his three scoring passes, an eight yarder. The scoreboard lights hadn't quit flickering before Baltimore's Marshall Johnson returned the ensuing kickoff 87 yards for a 17-14 Colts' lead. Moments later, Oakland's Ted Hendricks blocked a punt, setting up another scoring pass from the Snake to the Ghost, this time for 10 yards and a 21-17 Raider lead.

The fourth quarter became a matter of touchdown trading. After Bert Jones worked a Baltimore drive, Ron Lee scored from the one. Oakland responded similarly, with Pete Banazak getting the one-yard plunge for a 28-24 Oakland lead. Oakland coach John Madden went crazy on the sidelines over the next 78 seconds as Jones rushed the Colts back down the field to another touchdown, on a 13-yard run by Lee, for a 31-28 Baltimore lead with half the quarter to play.

Facing an uncertain end, Baltimore suddenly became tentative, and Stabler was anything but. With a hair under three minutes left, the Raiders got the ball back at their 30. By the two-minute warning, they had advanced to their own 44, where Madden called Ghost to the Post (Casper on a post pattern). The Colt secondary forced the path of the play to be altered from the left side of the field to the right, but Casper changed course and arrived just in time to pull Stabler's pass in over his shoulder, a picturesque catch for a 42-yard gain.

Three plays later, with 30 seconds left, the Raiders faced a fourth and one at the Baltimore five. Madden considered going for the win but didn't want to hinge his season on one running play. He opted for the tie and shot to win in overtime. He sent in nervous Errol Mann, who kicked the game-tying 22-yarder. Regulation ended at 31 all.

The scoring whirlwind died in the first overtime, then the Stabler-Casper routine resumed in the sixth period. Efficiently the Raiders moved downfield, where Casper went to the corner of the end zone and pulled in the 10-yard game winner. It was the worst kind of outcome for the Colts. They had been haunted and snakebitten.

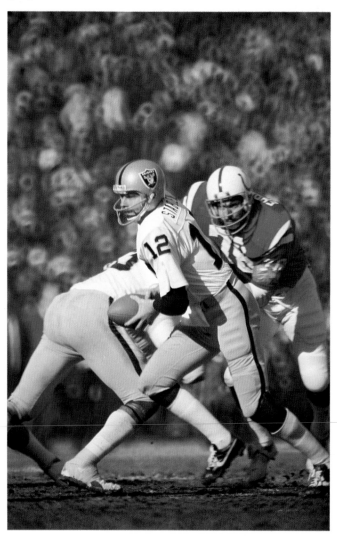

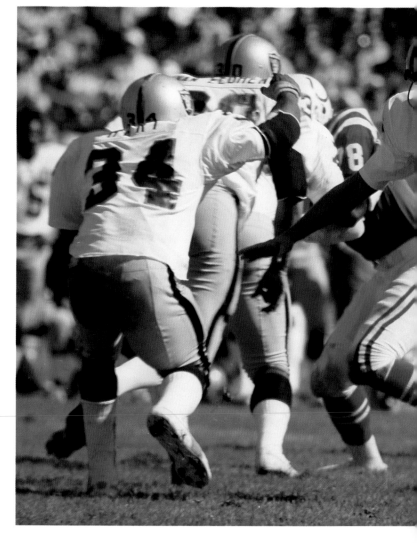

Earl's Run
Miami vs. Houston, 20 November 1978

It wasn't just another Monday Night Football game on 20 November 1978, when the Miami Dolphins traveled to the Astrodome to play the Houston Oilers. Both teams were in the heat of the playoff chase, trying to unseat the Pittsburgh Steelers as the AFC's dominant team. The Dolphins had the conference's leading rusher in Delvin Williams, and Houston rookie running back Earl Campbell was nipping at his heels.

Miami coach Don Shula figured the game would be an opportunity to see how his team would fare in the postseason. At the time, he didn't realize just how much of a look at the future he would get. Not only would the Oilers whip the Dolphins that night, they would also eliminate them from the playoffs a month later.

Beyond all that, the game is memorable because of Earl Campbell's 81-yard fourth quarter run. It was an incredible burst of acceleration by a leg-weary rookie on his twenty-eighth carry of the night. It froze the Dolphins in their comeback tracks. More impor-

Far left: Raider quarterback Ken Stabler tries to elude Baltimore's defensive linemen.
Left: Oakland's Ken Stabler, the 1973 and 1976 AFC passing leader, joined the Raiders in 1970.
Above: On 20 November 1978, the Oilers' Earl Campbell gained 199 yards in 28 carries and scored four touchdowns.

tant, it jettisoned Campbell toward the first of three consecutive NFL rushing crowns.

The Oiler defense had contained Williams' running but not the passing of Bob Griese, who completed 23 of 33 for 349 yards. Matching run for pass, the two teams exchanged touchdowns, one per team per quarter through the first three periods, to head into the fourth tied at 21. Campbell had scored two of Houston's first three scores. He continued that pace in the final period.

The Dolphins took the early lead, 23-21, when defensive end A J Duhe sacked Oiler quarterback Dan Pastorini in the end zone for a safety. But Campbell helped Houston motor the ball back down the field and finished the drive with a 12-yard scoring run for his third touchdown and a 28-23 Oiler lead.

Griese went right back to work with just under five minutes remaining, driving the Dolphins into scoring position. But Oiler safety Mike Reinfeldt deflected a Griese pass to linebacker Steve Kiner for an interception inside the Houston 10.

The Oilers needed to control the ball to win the game, but their main offensive weapon was a tired rookie. Campbell struggled to a first down at the 17. A short run netted him two more, then on second and 8 from the 19, the Oilers ran a sweep right.

'We knew he'd get the call,' Dolphin defensive end Doug Betters said afterward.

The play was designed for Campbell to swing to the right until he saw a break in the defense, then turn upfield hard. Dolphin safety Tim Foley blitzed and seemed close to dropping Campbell for a loss in the backfield. But Earl strode out of his clutch, then turned upfield, accelerated through an opening, and blazed 81 yards for the score.

Amazed reporters later asked Campbell how he could find such late-game strength. 'Ten more yards and I'd never have made it,' he confessed. On the night, he had gained 199 yards in 28 carries and scored four touchdowns. For three straight years, he would lead the NFL in rushing, piling up 1934 in 1980, accomplishment enough to place him among the greats.

Bradshaw Brightens Up
Dallas vs. Pittsburgh, Super Bowl XIII, January 1979

As if the intensity for Super Bowl XIII wasn't hot enough, Thomas 'Hollywood' Henderson, the Cowboys' outrageous linebacker, stirred the coals in the days before the game, announcing to the press that Pittsburgh quarterback Terry Bradshaw was so dumb he couldn't spell 'cat' if you spotted him the 'c' and the 'a.'

Bradshaw's response? Merely 318 yards and four touchdowns passing and the game's MVP trophy as the Steelers won, 35-31. The victory made them the first team in NFL history to win three Super Bowls (they would add a fourth the following year against the Los Angeles Rams). Afterward, Bradshaw basked in the locker room with a smile and told reporters, 'Go ask Henderson if I was dumb today.'

The game was hardly a masterpiece, rather a collector's item, a somewhat jazzed-up reprint of Pittsburgh's 21-17 victory over the Cowboys in Super Bowl X. Having beaten Denver soundly in Super Bowl XII, the Cowboys had seemed confident the 1979 outcome would be otherwise.

Dallas took the opening kickoff and moved to two quick first downs and excellent field position at the Pittsburgh 35. There Drew Pearson fumbled on a double reverse/pass option, and the Steelers recovered at their 47. Moments later, Bradshaw hit John Stallworth with the first of his touchdown passes for a 7-0 lead. The Steeler defense then seemed to have things under control until Bradshaw was sacked toward the end of the first quarter and fumbled in his own territory. Roger Staubach quickly cashed in the gift certificate with a 39-yard scoring pass to Tony Hill.

Then in the second quarter, the Dallas defense declared Doomsday again, as Henderson and fellow linebacker Mike Hegman sacked Bradshaw and strip-

Far left, top: Houston's Earl Campbell won his first of three consecutive NFL rushing crowns in 1978.
Far left: Quarterback Bob Griese completed 23 of 33 for 349 yards on 20 November 1978.
Left: Steeler quarterback Terry Bradshaw was elected MVP of Super Bowl XIII.
Above: The Cowboys' Tony Dorsett carries the ball during Super Bowl XIII.

ped him of the ball. Hegmen did the honors, running in for the score from 37 yards out to give Dallas a 14-7 edge.

Stallworth erased that minutes later when he pulled in a Bradshaw pass at the Pittsburgh 35, shook the tackle of safety Aaron Kyle and sprinted to the end zone, turning a routine pattern into a 75-yard score. Things continued to sour for the Cowboys on the following possession as Staubach threw an interception to Mel Blount. Bradshaw threw a seven-yarder to Rocky Bleier just before the half for a 21-14 Steeler lead.

The teams cooled considerably in the third, and the Dallas downslide continued. Jackie Smith, the former St Louis Cardinal tight end who had come out of retirement to bolster the Cowboys' lineup, dropped the tying touchdown pass. Dallas kicked a field goal on the next play and trailed, 21-17, going into the fourth. Then the downslide became an avalanche. Helped by a pass interference call, the Steelers drove deep, and Franco Harris scored on a 22-yard run. Next Dallas defensive lineman Randy White, who played on the kick return team, fumbled a short kickoff. Pittsburgh recovered, and Bradshaw threw 18 yards to Lynn Swann for a 35-17 lead with a little over six minutes left.

Above: Harris and fellow Steelers celebrate in the end zone after his fourth-quarter touchdown in Super Bowl XIII. *Right:* The Cowboys' Tony Hill is surrounded by Redskins during the final game of the 1979 season. Hill scored the tying touchdown and the conversion won his team the exciting game.

On the Steeler sidelines, the celebration began. Bradshaw saw Staubach trot onto the field and reminded his teammates that it was too early. Sure enough, the Cowboys drove 89 yards and scored to make it 35-24 with 2:27 left. Then they recovered the onside kick, and eight plays later, Staubach hit Butch Johnson with a four-yard pass for a 35-31 score with 0:22 on the clock.

This time, however, Bleier covered the onside kick, and Pittsburgh coach Chuck Noll had his third Super Bowl trophy. Henderson had difficulty holding back the tears of disappointment in the locker room. As for Bradshaw, he had a new three-letter word to spell: W-I-N.

Gunned Down
Dallas vs. Washington,
16 December 1979

Roger Staubach called Dallas' 35-34 come-from-behind win over Washington in December 1979 the most exciting game he ever played as a Cowboy. Better than four Super Bowls. Better than six NFC Championship games. Better, even, than Hail Mary. It must have been one heck of a game.

Better not, however, recall it within earshot of a Redskins fan. For them, the outcome was a black, bitter cud. Worse than the humiliating 38-9 loss to the Los Angeles Raiders in Super Bowl XVIII. Worse, even, than the 73-0 drubbing by the Chicago Bears in the 1940 NFL Championship.

Going into the final game of the 1979 season at Texas Stadium, both Washington and Dallas had 10-5 records. If the Redskins won the game, they had the NFC East title. If they lost, their season would end, because the Chicago Bears had a points advantage for the wild card spot.

The Redskins powered and finessed their way to a 17-0 second quarter lead, seemingly enough to put the game away. Even Staubach had never come back from such a deficit. Quarterback Joe Theisman had sneaked for one score and passed 55 yards to Benny Malone for another, and Mark Moseley had kicked a field goal.

The Cowboys didn't act like dead men, however. They calmly put together a scoring drive midway through the period, and then as time wound down, they added another, albeit a bit more frantically. With 0:09 on the clock, Staubach threw Preston Pearson a 26-yard touchdown pass. In Redskin retrospect, that was the killer. It set the stage for the Cowboys' third period drive to give them the lead, 21-17. Just as Redskins fans were about to get numb, Washington awakened with another 17-point outburst, beginning with a Moseley field goal. Then running back John Riggins closed out a drive with a one-yard scoring plunge just moments into the fourth period, and Washington had the lead again, 27-21.

With just under seven minutes left, Riggins worked his big, lumbering magic, a 66-yard touchdown run, setting up a seemingly insurmountable 34-21 lead. Washington's final challenge was the clock. The offense and defense worked together to chew it up. But with about three minutes left, running back Clarence Harmon fumbled, and Cowboy Randy White recovered. A mere 40 seconds later, Staubach threw a 26-yard touchdown pass to Ron Springs.

On the next series, the Redskins found themselves facing third and two at their own 33 with 2:27 left. Out of magic, big Riggins was dropped for a loss by defensive end Larry Cole, and Washington punted.

Trailing 34-28 with 1:47 on the clock, Staubach had a loaded shotgun and two timeouts left. Bad dream time for the Redskins. He used 60 seconds to get to the Washington eight. On the next play, he lofted the ball to Tony Hill in the end zone, just beyond the reach of defensive back Lemar Parrish. Rafael Septien's extra point was the winner, 35-34.

Staubach graciously left the Redskins 39 seconds to work a miracle. It wasn't enough, of course. Roger Staubach had a sweet, sweet memory for his old age. The Skins, well, they had next year.

Below: Dallas quarterback Roger Staubach prepares to pass. Staubach called his 16 December 1979 victory the most exciting game he has ever played.
Right: Tony Hill makes a leaping reception for Dallas.

THE EIGHTIES

Show Montana
The San Francisco 49ers vs. Dallas and Cincinnati

The San Francisco 49ers were the surprise of the NFC in 1981. Coach Bill Walsh had glued together quite a unit with an assortment of draft picks, free agents and trades. Finishing 2-14 in 1979, they surged to 13-3 over the 1981 regular season. The backbone of the team was an unsung defense, but the star of the show was quarterback Joe Montana. Since his college days at Notre Dame, he had shown a knack for coming back.

The playoffs that year offered ample opportunity to showcase the abilities of both facets of the 49ers' game – the unsung defense and Montana's come-from-behind, late-game heroics. In the end, both got their just rewards: Super Bowl rings.

Montana's big moment came against Dallas in the NFC Championship game played on 10 January 1982, although trivia buffs will recall he threw three interceptions that day. The two teams jumped back and forth until Dallas took a 17-4 lead just before the half on a Tony Dorsett sweep.

Things remained that way until the middle of the third quarter, when Cowboy quarterback Danny White threw an interception, which the 49ers used to set up the go-ahead touchdown, 21-17. Early in the fourth, Dallas tightened things up to 21-20 with a

Left: San Francisco's Dwight Clark kneels in the end zone after scoring the game-tying touchdown in the January 1982 NFC Championship game against Dallas, which his team then won on the conversion, 28-27.
Above: Cincinnati quarterback Ken Anderson prepares to pass in Super Bowl XVI.

Rafael Septien field goal. Then rookie running back Walt Easley fumbled for the 49ers, the Cowboys took over at midfield and four plays later White threw tight end Doug Cosbie a 21-yard touchdown pass for a 27-21 lead.

Montana was known as a confidence man, but he promptly deflated the 49ers' tires by throwing an interception on the next possession. Time for the San Francisco defense, which stopped the Cowboys' eat-the-clock plans and forced them to punt.

Show Montana got the ball back at the 49er 11-yard line with 4:54 left. Montana and Walsh wisely used the ground game to eat up the Cowboys' prevent defense. If they showed signs of tightening, Montana drilled a quick one to his primary receivers – Freddie Solomon and Dwight Clark.

The moment of truth came at the Dallas six on third and three with 58 seconds left. Montana was to look for Solomon in the left of the end zone, but the primary receiver was covered, and the Dallas rush, led by 6′ 9″ Ed 'Too Tall' Jones, was bearing down. So Montana exited to his right, bought just enough time, and lofted a high one, just as the Dallas boys crashed in. Dwight Clark, 6′ 4″, waiting at the back of the end zone, leaped up and grabbed the ball. Beautiful catch. Highlight films. The works. Ray Wersching's conversion put the 49ers in the Super Bowl, 28-27.

The unlikeliest of Super Bowl opponents – San Francisco and the Cincinnati Bengals – had the unlikeliest setting: the Pontiac Superdome. This time, the San Francisco defense took center stage – not that Montana and Clark and Solomon didn't do their part.

The game was simply won in the first three quarters on key defensive plays, particularly a goal-line stand in the third when Cincinnati quarterback Ken Anderson was leading his team back from a 20-0 deficit. After scoring a touchdown to narrow the lead to 20-7, Anderson completed a big pass on his next possession to Cris Collinsworth at the 49er 14. The Bengals then changed weapons to big fullback Pete Johnson and battered to a first down at the three.

Johnson then picked up two yards to the one, where the Bengals tried him again, this time over left guard. San Francisco lineman John Harty stopped him for no gain. Anderson then tried a pass, but was unable to find any open receiver in the end zone and had to settle for running back Charles Alexander at the one. Linebacker Dan Bunz hit him high and wrestled him down for no gain. The Bengals went again to Johnson on fourth down, but the 49er defensive line wasn't in the mood to give ground.

From the momentum of a tremendous goal line stand, San Francisco went on to win its first Super Bowl, 26-21.

All in A Name
Washington vs. Miami, Super Bowl XVII,
30 January 1983

In the early years of pro football, the stars were often immortalized by their nicknames. Red 'Galloping Ghost' Grange. Bronko Nagurski. Elroy 'Crazy Legs' Hirsch. Byron 'Whizzer' White. Sam 'Slingin' Sammy' Baugh. Johnny 'Blood' McNally. That, of course, was in the days before television, when athletes seemed larger than life.

Few such nicknames had survived in the glare of modern media. Super Joe Namath, perhaps. But not many more. Instead, the emphasis had shifted to group nicknames by the 1980s, as pro football dug into its heritage of hype. The result was a collision of monikers in Super Bowl XVII. The Killer Bees versus the Hawgs and Smurfs. Sounds like a bad Japanese horror flick. Rather, it was good old hard-nosed football, with a dash of Walt Disney.

The Killer Bees were the Miami Dolphins' stinging defense, so named because many of the starters – Lyle and Glenn Blackwood, Doug Betters, Bob Baumhower, Kim Bokamper, Bob Brudzinski – had last names starting with B. The Hawgs were Washington offensive linemen, dubbed such because they averaged 270 pounds and grunted opponents out of the way. The Smurfs were the Redskins' diminutive receivers, Alvin Garrett and Charlie Brown.

The 1982 regular season, shortened to nine games by a players' strike, had brought a rematch of the 1973 Super Bowl. After a decade, Don Shula was still the Dolphins' coach. But the Redskins had a new leader, Joe Gibbs, a purveyor of the passing game who instead came to rely on the run for the 30 January Super Bowl in Pasedena.

The reason for Gibbs' favoring the run was 32-year-old John Riggins, Washington's blend of power and speed at fullback. Riggins had sat out the 1980 season over a contract dispute. His comeback in 1981 had been a slow one. But he had been a major factor in the Skins' 8-1 regular season record in 1982. By the playoffs that year he was peaking and told Gibbs he should run the ball plenty. The coach listened, and in three playoff wins Riggins carried the ball 98 times for 444 yards, an average of more than 30 carries and 114 yards per game. In the Super Bowl he would surpass that, teaming with the Hawgs to become the battering ram that broke down Miami's defense.

The Dolphins scored first on a 76-yard bomb from quarterback David Woodley to Jimmy Cefalo. Washington answered with a Mark Moseley field goal. Miami then drove to a first down just inside the Washington 10, but the Redskin defense turned nasty. On fourth down, Uwe van Schamann kicked a field goal for a 10-3 lead. Theismann laced together a series of deceptive plays on an 80-yard drive, completed by a four-yard scoring pass to Garrett with just over two minutes left in the first half.

Left: The 49ers' punter Jim Miller gets off a good kick during Super Bowl XVI.

Below: Washington quarterback Joe Theismann hands off to John Riggins during Super Bowl XVII.

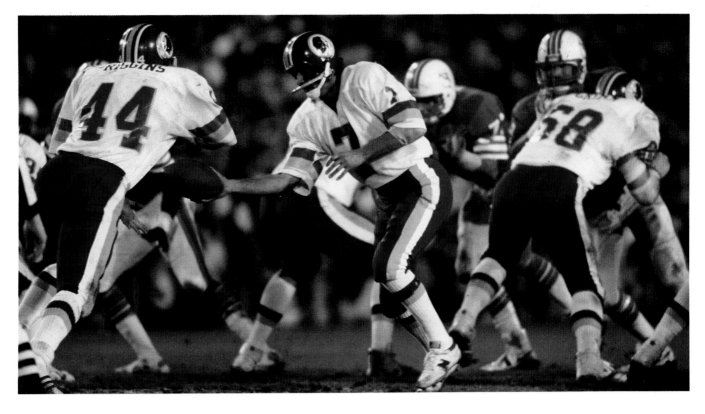

With the score tied at 10, Miami's receiving team struck back, freeing Fulton Walker on the return for a 98-yard touchdown. It was the only time that a kickoff had been returned for a touchdown in a Super Bowl. Washington rushed back down the field in the closing seconds of the half but ran out of time on the Miami 16, trailing 17-10.

In the third quarter, Moseley kicked another field goal, bringing the Redskins to 17-13. The Washington defense continued to dominate, holding the Dolphins' offense to almost nothing. It was the Miami defense that nearly put the game away with two minutes remaining in the period. Theismann was attempting a pass from his own 18 when Bokamper rushed in and tipped the ball. The big nose tackle was poised to catch the tip and run in for a score when Theismann alertly jumped in and knocked the ball away.

The fourth quarter would belong to Riggins and the Redskins. They were driving into Dolphin territory and faced a fourth and one at the Miami 43. Washington ran Riggins left and used a man in motion to draw cornerback Don McNeal away from the coverage area. Miami was in a six man line, and when McNeal realized the vulnerability he attempted to regain his position. But he slipped and was unable to get more than a hand on Riggins, which of course wasn't enough to stop Big John. 'Riggo's Run,' as the play became known, went for 43 yards and the go-ahead touchdown.

Ten minutes were left, and the Redskins used them running Riggins right at the Dolphins. They ate up the clock and digested another TD for a 27-17 victory, Washington's first championship since 1942.

Riggins had finished with 166 yards on 38 carries, which was MVP material and pretty near Hawg Heaven.

Jan Stenerud
Record Kicker, 12 December 1983
Green Bay vs. Tampa Bay

Jan Stenerud kicked field goals for the Kansas City Chiefs for 13 seasons, until just before the 1980 season when they released him. He bounced through tryouts with several teams before settling with the Green Bay Packers.

For three years, Stenerud led the league in kicking percentage, making better than 80 percent of his field goal attempts. By the 1983 season, Stenerud, a Norwegian, needed just 19 field goals to break George Blanda's NFL record of 335.

As the season progressed, he added three-pointers in the best possible way – helping his team to win. In the first game against Houston, he kicked two, including one in overtime to give the Packers a 41-38 victory. Two games later, Stenerud defeated the Los Angeles Rams, after running back Eric Dickerson fumbled, giving the Packers the opportunity to kick a 36-yarder for a 27-24 win.

Next, he kicked the winner in a wild Monday night game with the Washington Redskins. With 54 seconds left, he knocked up a 20-yarder, his second field goal of the game, for a 48-47 Green Bay victory. Then, seven games later, he defeated the Chicago Bears on the game's final play with a 19-yarder.

Going into the next week's Monday night game against Tampa Bay, Stenerud needed just two kicks to break Blanda's record. The first, a 35-yarder, came in the first quarter. Then he broke the record with a 32-yarder in the second quarter, giving the Packers a 6-3 lead. Tampa Bay scored a touchdown but missed the extra point, leaving the score 9-6 and setting up a dramatic finish to Stenerud's record-breaking night.

On the last series of the game, Green Bay drove into field goal range, and with time running out, Stenerud kicked a 23-yard goal to tie the game at 9. Then he won it in overtime, with yet another 23-yarder, his fourth of the night and three hundred thirty-seventh of his career. The game was the fifth he had won for Green Bay that season. At age 41, after 17 pro seasons, he had worked his way to the top.

Left: The Redskins' big fullback, John Riggins, coasts into the end zone after scoring the 43-yard go-ahead touchdown in Super Bowl XVII, against the Dolphins. With 166 yards on 38 carries, Riggins won Super Bowl MVP honors.
Top right: Green Bay's kicker, Jan Stenerud, chats with on the sidelines. Stenerud broke George Blanda's NFL field goal record, and won the game in overtime, on 12 December 1983.
Right: Jan Stenerud kicks for a field goal.

1984
A Smashing Season

The 1984 NFL season was a time for smashing records, any kind of record – passing, rushing, receiving – and most of the big ones fell:

★ The Chicago Bears' Walter Payton bypassed Jim Brown's record for career rushing yardage of 12,312 yards. By season's end, Payton had 13,309 and was well on his way beyond 15,000, a territory uncharted.

★ Miami quarterback Dan Marino threw for 48 touchdown passes, blowing right by Y A Tittle's single season total of 36, and passed for 5084 yards, becoming the first player to go beyond 5000 yards.

★ Mark Clayton, Marino's prime target, caught 19 touchdown passes, breaking the record of 17 set by Don Hutson, Elroy Hirsch and Bill Groman.

★ Los Angeles Rams' running back Eric Dickerson beat O J Simpson's single-season rushing record of 2003 yards (in 14 games) by piling up 2105 in 16 games. Simpson's record for combined yardage, 2243 all-purpose yards in 1975, also fell to Dickerson by a single yard, 2244.

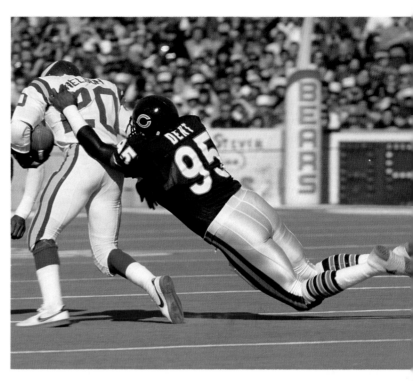

Left: The Bears' defensive end Richard Dent makes a leaping tackle. Dent led his team in 1984 with 17 and a half sacks.
Below: Charger Charlie Joiner stretches to make the catch. Joiner finished the 1984 season with a record 657 career receptions.
Right: Washington's Art Monk makes a leaping catch. Monk's 106 receptions in 1984 set a new season record.

★ In the receiving department, Washington's Art Monk caught 106 passes, breaking Charley Hennigan's record 101 catches for Houston in 1964. And Charlie Joiner of San Diego claimed the lead in career receptions, finishing with 657, well ahead of Charley Taylor's 649 catches.

★ The Bears' defense set a record with 72 quarterback sacks. Defensive end Richard Dent had 17 and a half sacks to lead the team.

★ The San Francisco 49ers set a record of regular season wins by going 15-1. The 49ers also showed the sports world a thing or two in the Super Bowl by shutting down Miami's grand passing attack.

Regardless of who took home the trophy, it was obvious to just about everyone that with the 1984 season pro football had moved into a new age. New records, new dimensions, new heroes.

But just as the game was set to take off for destinations unknown, the Chicago Bears started a back-to-the-basics movement, and crunched the league in 1985 with defense. Playing good old hard-nosed football, the Bears blew by their opponents and squashed the New England Patriots in Super Bowl XX. George Halas and Vince Lombardi were smiling somewhere. 'Football is blocking and tackling,' Lombardi said once. 'Everything else is mythology.'

So it is.

Below: San Francisco's stellar quarterback, Joe Montana. Montana's 49ers went 15-1 in 1984, and capped a strong season by taking home Super Bowl rings.
Right: Dolphin quarterback Dan Marino threw a record 48 touchdown passes in 1984.

Lucky 21

As much as any season, the 1986 playoffs leading up to Super Bowl XXI had their moments. For the AFC, the crucial games were stomach twisters, ending with sudden death. In the NFC, the mood was a performance of domination. Throughout, the proceedings rode on the arms of young quarterbacks. Each of them – New York's Phil Simms, Cleveland's Bernie Kosar and Denver's John Elway – contributed to the game's bankroll of legends.

For Kosar, the moment came in the Browns' first-round playoff match with the New York Jets at Cleveland Stadium. Kosar had thrown few interceptions during the regular season, but in the fourth quarter against the Jets, he had thrown two, both leading to New York scores. With 4:08 left in regulation, the Browns were down, 20-10, when Kosar started the offense again. Many fans were leaving, but the Dawgs, Cleveland's wild bleacher fans, only increased their taunting of the Jets' weary defense. Even the high spirits couldn't have lifted the home team moments later when a holding penalty and a sack placed the ball at their own 18.

Facing second and 24, Kosar dropped back to pass and was roughed by Jets' defensive end Mark Gastineau. From there, Kosar zipped four straight first-down passes to Brian Brennan and Reggie Langhorne to place the ball at the New York three, where running back Kevin Mack scored. With 1:57 left, the Browns were down, 20-17, with two timeouts remaining.

The Jets covered the onsides kick but couldn't get a first down, and Kosar got one more chance at his own 33 with 0:51 on the clock. First there was a pass interference call on Jets' back Carl Howard, then a 37-yard completion for receiver Webster Slaughter, who ran to the Jets' five with 25 seconds left. Kosar tried an end zone pass, which was just beyond Slaughter and almost intercepted by Russell Carter. With 11 seconds left, Cleveland coach Marty Schottenheimer sent in veteran placekicker Mark Moseley,

Below: The Browns' offense moves downfield in the 1986 AFC playoff against the Jets. The Browns came from behind to win on a Mark Moseley field goal in double overtime.
Right: Cleveland's quarterback Bernie Kosar throws for a gain during the 1986 AFC playoff.

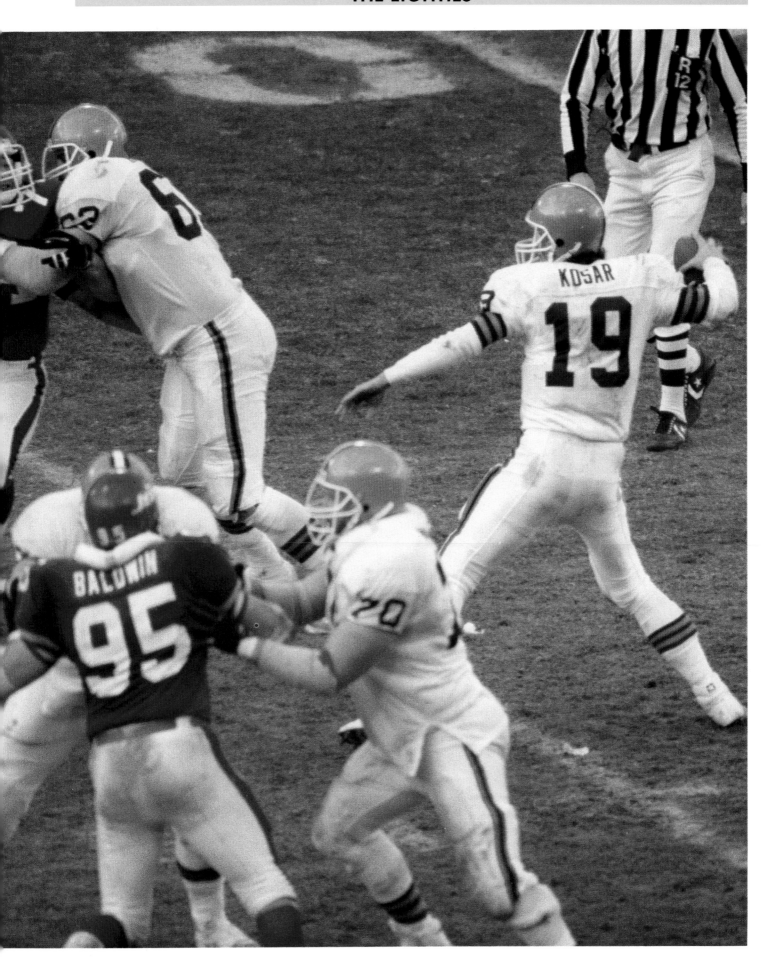

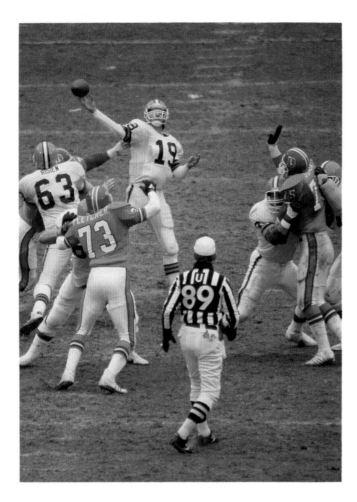

Above: The Browns' Bernie Kosar lofts a pass during the 1986 AFC Championship against the Broncos.
Right: Fans jam the stadium to witness the Broncos' come-from-behind overtime victory in the 1986 AFC Championship.

who had been acquired after being cut by the Washington Redskins. Moseley kicked the tying field goal, sending the game to its first overtime.

When the Jets failed on the first possession of overtime, Kosar again drove the Browns down to the Jets' five, a chip shot for Moseley. Only he missed, and the game dragged into the second overtime, where finally with 2:02 left, Moseley connected with a 27-yarder to win, 23-20. The Cleveland fans, who had not witnessed a playoff victory in umpteen years, carried their celebration right up to the closing minutes of the next week's game with Denver, where Elway killed the Browns and quieted the Dawgs with a similar comeback.

The Browns had appeared headed to the Super Bowl with just under six minutes left when Kosar passed to Brennan, who scampered past Bronco safety Dennis Smith for a 48-yard touchdown and a 20-13 Cleveland lead. It seemed even more certain moments later when Denver muffed the kickoff and began a drive on its own two.

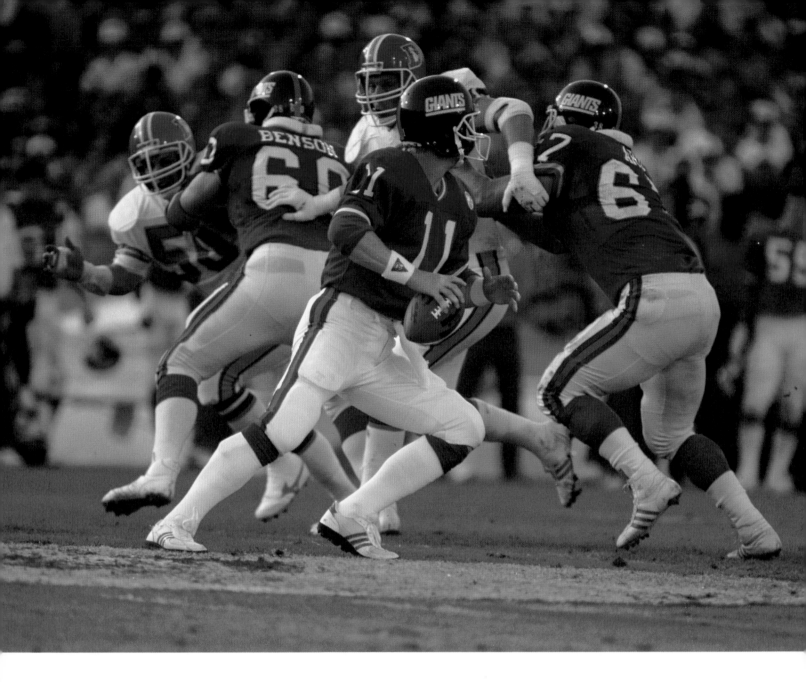

Elway entered the huddle and smiled, saying to his teammates, 'Good things happen if you work hard.' Sure, the Broncos had barely gained a yard throughout the fourth quarter. But the afternoon's swirling snow had stopped, and the Denver offense suddenly started. Elway threw a short pass to Sammy Winder, then ran for 11 yards three plays later. Next came a 22-yard bullet to Steve Sewell, followed by a 12-yard completion to Steve Watson.

An incompletion and an eight-yard sack left third and long, which Elway converted into a 20-yard gain to Mark Jackson at the Browns' 28. He topped that with a 14-yarder to Sewell and a nine-yard run to the Cleveland five. With 39 seconds left, Elway lined a strike to Jackson angling across the middle of the end zone. Karlis' placement completed the miracle drive, 20-20. When the Browns failed the sudden-death test, Karlis punched up a 33-yarder, and the Broncos were headed to the Super Bowl.

There, they sustained their magic against the favored New York Giants through the first quarter. Elway ran and passed the Broncos to a 10-7 lead, but

Above: New York Giants' quarterback Phil Simms prepares to throw in Super Bowl XXI. On the way to leading his team to a 39-20 victory over the Broncos, Simms captured the MVP honors.
Right: Bengals' nose tackle Tim Krumrie is taken off the field by stretcher after breaking his leg early in the first quarter of Super Bowl XXIII.

shortly thereafter, the Denver momentum died when Karlis missed two field goals and New York sacked Elway in the end zone for a safety. Simms then took his turn as the quarterback of the hour, completing a record 22 of 25 passes to lead the Giants in a 39-20 rout. The Giants' defense, led by linebacker Lawrence Taylor, had captured the headlines all season.

There was little doubt, however, about the Super Bowl MVP. Simms all the way. 'Phil had this strange sort of glow,' said Giants' coach Bill Parcells. 'It was like he was in a perfect biorhythm stage or something.'

The win gave the Giants their first championship since 1956. Simmply wonderful.

Walsh Goes Out a Winner
San Francisco vs. Cincinnati,
Super Bowl XXIII,
22 January 1989

In the 1988 season, Coach Bill Walsh led his San Francisco 49ers to the Super Bowl for the third time in the decade, but it was far from a romp. The 'Niners had limped through the first two-thirds of the season, as injuries to quarterback Joe Montana and nonpareil receiver Jerry Rice put the attack load on versatile runner Roger Craig. Then, as health returned, the team won its last five regular season games and steamed through postseason wins over Minnesota and Chicago.

Cincinnati took a more sure-footed route to Super Bowl XXIII, opening with six straight wins, holding off a challenge from Cleveland, and then disposing of Seattle and Buffalo in the playoffs. Quarterback Boomer Esiason, the American Conference MVP, had a host of weapons to call upon: fast receivers Tim McGee and Eddie Brown, breakaway runner James Brooks, and sensational rookie fullback Ickey Woods. But Coach Sam Wyche's Bengals were considered suspect on defense, and San Francisco was favored.

Set for Miami's Joe Robbie Stadium, Super Bowl XXIII brought a rematch of Super Bowl XVI. But whereas that affair had seen San Francisco jump off to a big first-half lead, Cincinnati served notice that this game would be different by doing what none of the 75,179 in attendance expected – playing tight defense. Their task was made all the more difficult when star nose tackle Tim Krumrie suffered a freak broken leg early in the first quarter. The stomach-churning break, shown again and again in replay on TV, resulted from Krumrie's own momentum rather than the action of any other player. Despite the absence of their top defensive player, the Bengals held San Francisco in check throughout the first half, limiting the high-powered 49ers to Mike Cofer's 41-yard field goal in the opening quarter. Cincinnati matched that with Jim Breech's 34-yarder in the second period, and, for the first time in history, a Super Bowl game was tied at halftime.

The third quarter saw more tough defense. Breech put Cincinnati in front, 6-3, with a 43-yard field goal. But linebacker Bill Romanowski intercepted an Esiason pass at the 23, and four plays later Cofer tied the game again from 32 yards out. The deadlock lasted only until Cincinnati's Stanford Jennings tucked the ensuing kickoff under his arm at the seven and raced 93 electrifying yards to the game's first touchdown.

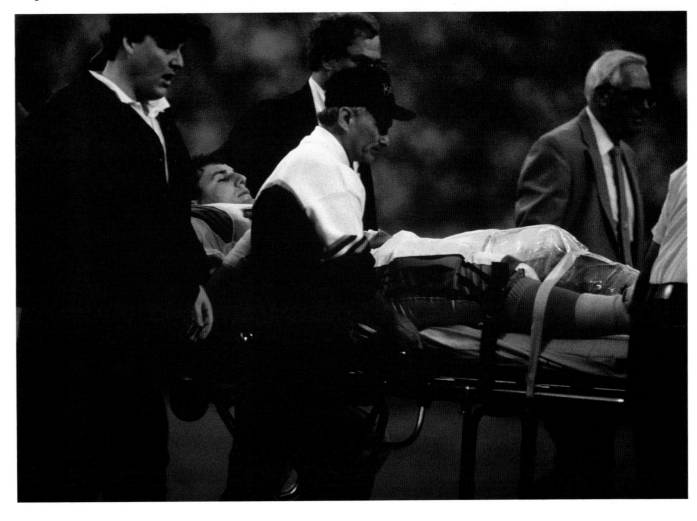

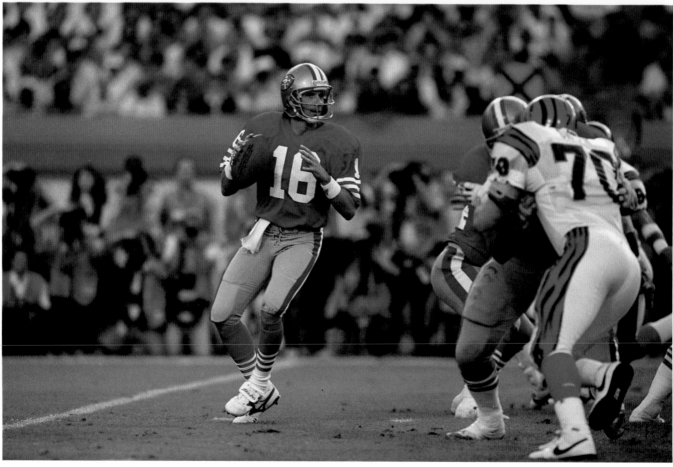

That seemed to wake up the comatose San Francisco offense for the fourth quarter. Starting at his own 15, Montana threw to Rice for 31 yards and to Craig for 40. His third pass went straight to Bengal cornerback Lewis Billups in the end zone, but the overanxious defender dropped the ball. After that reprieve, Montana found Rice for a touchdown to tie the game again.

A few moments later Cofer tried a long kick from the Cincinnati 49, but it sailed wide, giving Wyche's men good field position. The Bengals drove down to the 49ers' 22, and the reliable Breech kicked his third field goal of the day. Cincinnati held a 16-13 lead with only 3:20 left on the clock.

Montana was the master of the last-ditch drive, but he had his work cut out for him when the kickoff left his team at its own eight. Short passes to John Frank and Rice moved the ball to the 35. A 17-yard toss to Rice put San Francisco in Cincinnati territory, and a 13-yarder to Craig got them to the 35. A 10-yard penalty set them back, but the Bengals' defense was tired and Rice, who would be named game MVP, was open at will. Montana zinged one over the middle to the slanting Rice. Before he was hauled down, the great receiver was at the 18 on the key play of the game. With everybody on the Cincinnati side chasing Rice, Montana picked up eight yards on a short pass to Craig. Then he completed his game-winning, 92-yard drive with a 10-yard touchdown throw to his other wide receiver, John Taylor.

The victory was the last as 49ers' coach for Walsh, who gave up his clipboard to join NBC as an analyst. But the next season, under George Seifert, Montana, Rice, Craig and the rest cemented San Francisco's claim as the Team of the Decade with a fourth Super Bowl ring.

Top left: The Bengals' Stanford Jennings breaks through 49ers' tackles during his 93-yard touchdown kickoff return in Super Bowl XXIII.
Bottom left: San Francisco's quarterback Joe Montana prepares to pass to his favorite receiver, Jerry Rice.
Left: The 49ers' Jerry Rice leaps up to make this fourth-quarter catch in Super Bowl XXIII.

Overleaf: Wide receiver John Taylor caught the winning 10-yard touchdown pass. This play capped a 92-yard drive and another San Francisco Super Bowl championship.

THE NINETIES

Two Feet Wide of Glory
New York Giants vs. Buffalo, Super Bowl XXV, 29 January 1991

The NFL scheduled the Silver Anniversary Super Bowl XXV for Tampa Bay, but it turned out to be the first trans-New York State Super Bowl when the Buffalo Bills and New York Giants made it to the finale. Both teams sported strong defenses. The Bills were led by defensive end Bruce Smith and linebackers Cornelius Bennett and Shane Conlan. The Giants, who held foes to a league-low 211 points, boasted their own star linebackers in Pepper Johnson, Carl Banks and all-time great Lawrence Taylor. In the NFC title game they stuffed defending champion San Francisco's bid for a third consecutive Super Bowl by limiting them to a single touchdown and two field goals.

But the Bills' and Giants' offenses were as different as an Uzi and a flintlock. High-tech Buffalo's devastating 'no-huddle' attack whipsawed opponents with Thurman Thomas's wide-ranging slashes and Jim Kelly's deep passes to speedy receivers Andre Reed and James Lofton. In the AFC Championship game, Coach Marv Levy's Bills buried the Raiders, 51-3.

The Giants' attack, conservative before regular quarterback Phil Simms was knocked out with a foot injury in Game 14, became even more so when seven-year backup Jeff Hostetler replaced him. Then Rodney Hampton, the team's best runner, suffered a broken

Below: Super Bowl XXV MVP Ottis Anderson powers his way through the Bills' defensive line.

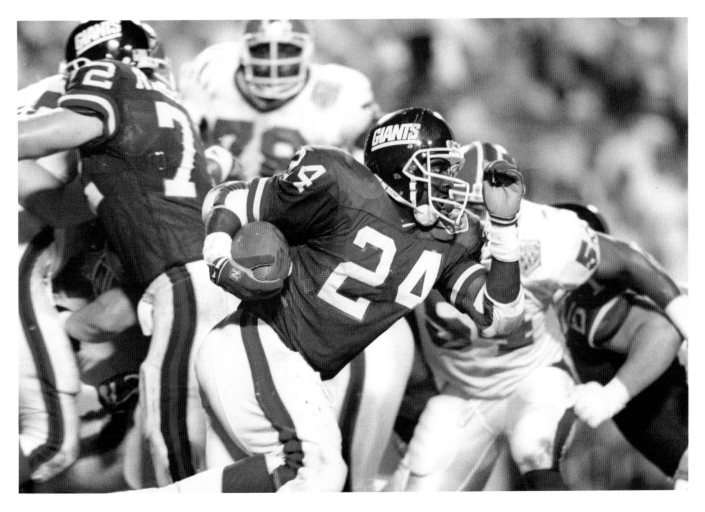

leg in the first playoff game, and Coach Bill Parcells's offense became positively spartan. Against the 49ers, New York survived on Hostetler's short, safe passes and the up-the-gut rushes of veteran Ottis Anderson. But, significantly, all the Giants' points in that game came on Matt Bahr field goals.

Both New York and Buffalo showed what they did best in the Super Bowl's opening quarter. The Giants drove 58 yards in bits and pieces to Bahr's 28-yard field goal. Then Kelly outdid the Giants' drive in one play, throwing a 61-yard bomb to Lofton to set up a game-tying, 23-yard field goal by Scott Norwood. Before the period ended, the Bills launched a drive from their own 20 that culminated early in the second quarter in Don Smith's one-yard touchdown run. A few moments later, Bruce Smith caught Hostetler in the end zone for a safety.

Leading 12-3 with their offense in high gear, Buffalo seemed to have the Giants on the run. But

Left: Speedy wide receiver James Lofton caught this 61-yard pass, which led to a field goal for Buffalo.
Below: The Bills' quarterback Jim Kelly led the 'no-huddle' offense for Buffalo.
Right: Backup quarterback Jeff Hostetler followed the Giants' game plan by orchestrating long time-consuming drives that kept the Bills' explosive offense cold and off the field.

Taylor and company cooled the Bills' attack. With 3:49 left in the half, the Giants regrouped at their own 13. Hostetler mixed short passes with the running of Anderson and Dave Meggett in a 10-play drive that consumed 87 yards and all but 25 seconds of the clock. His 14-yard bullseye to Stephen Baker left New York trailing only 12-10 at the half.

The Giants opened the second half with another monster drive of 75 yards. Anderson broke away for a 25-yard run on one play, but most of the yardage was accomplished in typical nickle-and-dime chunks. By the time Anderson hauled his 33-year-old body across the goal line for a go-ahead touchdown, New York had run 14 plays and used up 9:29 of the clock. Meanwhile, the Giants defense had rested and the Buffalo offense had gotten cold.

The Bills took the rest of the third quarter to get going. But with about a minute left, Parcells stretched his luck too far and Anderson was stopped by Bruce

Below: Scott Norwood's field goal attempt, with eight seconds left in the game, misses the mark by two feet. The Giants defeat the Bills in Super Bowl XXV by the score of 20-19.

Smith on a fourth-and-two at the Buffalo 35. Kelly moved the Bills downfield on a 19-yard toss to Kenneth Davis. Then on the first play of the final period, Thomas burst off right tackle for 31 yards and a touchdown to put Buffalo back in front, 19-17.

Now it was the Giants' turn on the seesaw. This time Hostetler targeted his tight end Mark Bavaro, who had been almost unused till now. Three times he hit Bavaro with key passes as the Giants ran off still another long, time-consuming drive – 74 yards and 7½ minutes. From the 21, Bahr zeroed in on his second field goal of the day to give the Giants the lead again, 20-19.

Buffalo was anything but dead, but after one false start, they were 90 yards away with 2:16 on the clock and only one timeout in the till. On third-and-one at the 19, Thomas broke loose for 22 yards up the right side. Kelly and Thomas took Buffalo 30 more yards, but time was almost gone. With eight seconds left, Norwood set up for a do-or-die field goal attempt at the New York 47. The ball was snapped, Norwood kicked, the ball arched high and faded wide right by only two feet. Giants win!

INDEX

INDEX

Picture Credits
Allsport USA: Stephen Dunn, 92, 93 (bottom); Mike Powell 87, 88 (right), 89, 90; Rick Stewart 88 (left), 91, 93 (right), 94.
Chicago Bears: pages 8, 9 (bottom)
Focus on Sports: pages 2-3, 6, 7, 50 (both), 51 (both), 53 (bottom), 54-55 (both), 57 (both), 59 (all three), 60, 61 (both), 62-63 (both), 64, 65 (both), 66-67 (all three), 68 (both), 69 (both), 70, 71, 72 (both), 73 (both), 74, 75, 76, 77 (both), 78-79 (all three), 80-81 (both), 82, 83, 84-85 (both), 86.
Pro-Football Hall of Fame: pages 9 (top), 12 (both), 40 (top left), 42 (top right).
UPI/Bettmann Newsphotos: pages 1, 4-5, 10, 11 (both), 13 (both), 14 (both), 15 (both), 16 (both), 17, 18 (both), 19 (all three), 20, 21, 22 (both), 23 (all three), 24-25, 26 (both), 27, 28, 29 (both), 30 (both), 31 (both), 32, 33 (both), 34 (both), 35, 36, 37 (both), 38-39 (all three), 40 (bottom left and top right), 40-41, 41 (right), 42 (top left and bottom), 42-43, 42 (right), 44, 45, 46 (both), 47 (both), 48, 49 (both), 52, 53 (top), 56 (all three), 58.

Acknowledgments
The author and publisher would like to thank the following people who have helped in the preparation of this book: Adrian Hodgkins, who designed it; Barbara Paulding Thrasher, who edited it; Donna Cornell Muntz and Jean Chiaramonte Martin, who did the picture research; and Florence Norton, who prepared the index.